Straits Settlements Law Reports V2: 1894

W. J. Naples

1894

STRAITS SETTLEMENTS

LAW REPORTS.

Published under the direction of the Committee of the Singapore Bar.

WITH THE

Approval of the Judges of the Supreme Court.

1894.—Vol. II.

EDITOR	W. J. NAPIER, Esq.
ASSISTANT EDITOR	SONG ONG SIANG, Esq.
EDITOR IN PENANG	F. J. C. ROSS, Esq.
EDITOR IN MALACCA	S. R. GROOM, Esq.

SINGAPORE.

PRINTED AND PUBLISHED FOR THE COMMITTEE OF THE SINGAPORE BAR.

A TABLE.

OF THE

NAMES OF THE CASES REPORTED

IN THIS VOLUME.

JUDGES OF THE SUPREME COURT
OF THE
STRAITS SETTLEMENTS.

The Honourable W. H. L. COX ... ... *Chief Justice.*

The Honourable S. H. GATTY ... ... *Puisne Judge.*

The Honourable A. F. G. LAW ... ... *Puisne Judge.*

*The Honourable W. R. COLLYER ... ... *Puisne Judge.*

Attorneys-General.

The Honourable W. R. COLLYER.   †The Honourable T. H. KERSHAW.

Solicitor-General.

D. LOGAN, Esq.

Bar Committee. Singapore.

The Honourable A. L. DONALDSON, M.L.C., *Hon. Secretary.*

W. NANSON, Esq.

W. J. NAPIER, Esq.

---

* Was appointed Acting Puisne Judge on the 27th of October 1894.
† Was appointed Acting Attorney-General on the 27th of October 1894

Table of Cases Cited.

INDEX.

In re RIBEIRO'S-BILL OF SALE.

[SINGAPORE.]

Bills of Sale Ordinance 1886—Pre-existing debt.

Section 8 (3) of The Bills of Sale Ordinance 1886 cannot be evaded by the passing and repassing of money. A party to a Bill of Sale is not estopped by the statement of consideration expressed therein from shewing that a pre-existing debt was the real consideration.

BONSER, C. J.

1893
Aug. 28.

BY a Bill of Sale dated the 23rd day of December 1892. in the Statutory form, and duly registered, M. Ribeiro mortgaged certain chattels to M.R.M.A. Raman Chitty for securing $300 and interest. The consideration was expressed to be " the sum of $300 now paid."

At the date of the Bill of Sale M. Ribeiro owed M.R M.A. Mootiah Chitty the sum of $270 for rent. Raman Chitty was the successor of Mootiah Chitty in the management of the firm M.R.M.A. and this rent of $270 was really due to the firm. and not to Mootiah Chitty as an individual. At the date of the Bill of Sale, Raman Chitty was acting as such manager and held a power of attorney from Mootiah. The Bill of Sale was also taken by Raman Chitty on behalf of his firm. The $300 was paid in cash on the execution of the Bill of Sale, and the same day $270 was returned to Raman Chitty in payment of the rent. Ribeiro also stated that the balance $30 was also returned for interest &c., but Raman Chitty denied this. Ribeiro applied by Summons under Section 10 (3) of the Bills of Sale Ordinance 1886 to restrain Raman Chitty from selling under the Bill of Sale, on the ground that the Bill of Sale was void, being made in consideration of a pre-existing debt. The Judge in Chambers dismissed the application.

From this dismissal Ribeiro appealed.

BONSER, C. J.

1893.

In re
RIBEIRO'S
BILL OF SALE.

W. Nanson, for Appellant, moved.

[*BONSER. C. J.* The words "No longer" in Section 10 (3) imply that there was formerly a cause of seizure. It is doubtful whether the Court can make the order asked for under the circumstances.]

Nanson cites *Expte Cotton* (L.R. 11 Q.B.D. 301) and *Expte Bolland* (L. R. 21 Ch. D. 543.)

[*BONSER, C. J.* suggested that respondent should waive the objection and consent to the validity of the Bill of Sale being tried on this application. This course was adopted.]

Nanson.—The Bill of Sale was given to secure in part $270 then due and owing by the grantor to the grantee and not in consideration of any advance. Being given for a pre-existing debt under Section 8 (3) the bill of sale is void.

Then the consideration was not truly stated. There was in reality no advance at all. Upon the facts the whole transaction was a sham. There could be no advance at all if in pursuance of a prior arrangement the $300 paid to the grantor was directly afterwards returned to the grantee. In *Exparte National Mercantile Bank* (15 Ch. D. at p 53) James L J. says. "of course if there was a bargain that the whole sum which is stated to be the consideration should be at once returned to the grantee, that would be a sham transaction, and the Court would know how to deal with it."

Sisson.—For Respondent.

The consideration was the $300 actually paid. and not the antecedent debt. The transaction was genuine and not a sham. The respondent had a right to distrain for the rent, and had therefore a stronger position than that which he afterwards acquired under the Bill of Sale. He would not enter into a sham transaction in order to weaken his position. Section 8 (3) does not appear in the English Act. but the English decisions on the section as to true statement of consideration are in point. If the consideration is "truly stated" in this Bill of Sale, then the true consideration is the $300 cash as stated and cannot be the pre-existing debt. In *Davies v. Usher.* (L. R. 12 Q. B. D. 490,) £30 was actually paid on execution and £15 returned at once, yet the Bill of Sale was held valid. notwithstanding section 12 of the Act.

[*BONSER, C. J.* The Court in that case held that there was no evidence that the transaction was a sham. If the facts here shew the contrary that case is not an authority.

Sisson. The agreement to repay the rent out of the consideration money is merely a collateral agreement as to the application of the money when received; and does not form part of the consideration *Exparte National Mercantile Bank.* (L. R. 15 Ch D. 42) In that case, Bramwell L. J. says (page 57) "Take the case of a bill of "sale of farming stock given for £100, there being an agreement that "out of the £100 the grantor should pay the grantee £40 which he "owes him for a particular horse which he had purchased of "him, is it conceivable that the act would require that the "agreement to pay for the horse should be stated in the "deed? *In that case the £100 would clearly be the consideration for* "*the bill of sale.*" In *Thomas v. Searles* (L. R. [1891,] 2 Q. B. 408), a debtor who owed a sum of money partly secured by an existing bill of sale, executed a second bill of sale of the same chattels to secure a fresh advance, on the understanding that out of the sum advanced he should pay off the existing debt. The bill of sale was expressed to be made in consideration of the fresh advance, without alluding to the intended application of the money. The money was actually paid to the grantor and applied by him as agreed and it was held that the consideration was truly stated, and the Bill of Sale valid accordingly.

The two last cases shew that in the present instance the consideration is truly stated, or in other words that the true consideration is the $300, and not the pre-existing debt.

The Appellant is estopped from denying the truth of the statement in the Bill of Sale itself that the consideration was the $300. Section 92 of the Evidence Ordinance is the only provision under which the Appellant can contradict his deed, and there is no question of "illegality" or "want of consideration" in this case.

Pre-existing debt means a debt owing to the grantee and not to another person. In this case it was owing to Mootiah Chitty and not to Raman Chitty.

[*BONSER, C. J.* The debt was owing to the same firm in both cases.]

W. Nanson in reply.

BONSER, C. J. The objection taken by the grantor is that the Bill of Sale was made in consideration of a pre-existing debt. The

BONSER, C. J. facts are that the grantor was indebted to the grantee for rent and
1893.
IN re
RIBEIRO'S
BILL OF SALE.
the grantee was pressing him for payment, and for some reason or
other the grantee thought a Bill of Sale more satisfactory than the
mere right to distrain and as the grantee charged interest on the
arrears of rent which could not be distrained for, it may have been for
this reason that he preferred to take a Bill of Sale. This disposes
of the argument that by abandoning his right to distrain and taking
a Bill of Sale he got no benefit. The Bills of Sale Ordinance differs
from the English Act. It invalidates Bills of Sale given in consideration of a pre-existing debt, and the question I have to decide is, was
the Bill of Sale given wholly or in part, in consideration of a pre-
existing debt. There is an affidavit by the grantor that the grantee
threatened proceedings unless he got a Bill of Sale, and that the
amount of the alleged consideration was paid to the grantor and
afterwards returned to the grantee which is not denied by the grantee,
and he admits that that was the agreement between the parties. It was
not a bona fide transaction, it was intended that the consideration money
should be handed over to the grantor as a sham, and had the grantor
not pa'd it back he might have brought himself within reach of the
Criminal Law. It would not have been the act of an honest man if
he had declined to repay it. It is practically admitted that it was a
device to avoid the Bills of Sale Ordinance; and where the law for-
bids a thing and the parties agree to evade the law neither party is
estopped from showing that the consideration stated on the face of a
deed is not the true consideration, or that it is illegal, or in contraven-
tion of any Statute.

Order made in Chambers reversed and order made restraining the grantee from exercising his power of Sale.

Solicitors for Grantor.—*Rodyk & Davidson.*

Solicitor for Grantee.—*A. J. Sisson.*

NOOR MOHAMED v. ALAMALOO.

[SINGAPORE.]

Practice—Court of Requests—Power to grant new Trial.

The Commissioner of a Court of Requests, having heard and determined
a suit, is *functus officio* and cannot rehear it.

BONSER, C. J.
1893.
Aug. 29.
THIS was an application under section 20 of the Civil Appeals
Ordinance, 1893, asking for the review of an order of C. W.

S. Kynnersley, Esq., Commissioner of the Court of Requests at Singapore, by which he gave judgment in favour of the defendant in a suit in which Noor Mohamed was plaintiff, and Alamaloo, defendant. The plaintiff having proved service of the summons upon the defendant, obtained judgment against her, she not appearing when the case came on for hearing. The defendant subsequently applied for a re-hearing of the case, and the Commissioner made an order for a new trial, and, subsequently, after re-hearing it, gave judgment in favour of the defendant.

BONSER. C. J.

1893.

NOOR MOHAMED
v.
ALAMALOO.

The only question raised by the present appeal was as to whether the Commissioner, having once heard and given judgment in a suit, could afterwards re-hear it.

Khory appeared for the Appellant.

Logan (Acting A. G.) on the suggestion of Bonser C. J. that the matter was one of public importance, argued on behalf of the Respondent, who appeared in person.

BONSER, C. J.

The Courts of Requests were established under the Charter of 1855, which provides that it was to be lawful for the Court of Directors and for the President or Governor in Council of Prince of Wales Island, Singapore and Malacca, to establish Courts for the recovery of small debts, and for the trial of suits where the debt or matter in dispute does not exceed $32 ; and also to frame such other rules or regulations for the due administration of justice in such Courts as they think fit. This enabled the Indian Government to establish Courts of Requests and to form rules and regulations suitable to the various classes of suitors. The first legislative enactment dealing with these Courts is the Indian Act XXIX of 1866. That Act recites the power contained in the Charter to establish Courts of Requests, and that such Courts had been established at Penang, Province Wellesley, Singapore, and Malacca ; and that it was expedient to enlarge their jurisdiction from $32 to $50. This Act does not in any way empower the Courts of Requests to grant a new trial. In December, 1866, the Governor in Council, acting under the Charter of 1855, repealed all proclamations, orders, rules, and regulations, relating to Courts of Requests, theretofore issued, and drew up and promulgated certain rules and regulations which were intended as a full code of procedure. The Courts Ordinance, of 1878, enumerates as one of the local Courts, for

BONSER, C. J. the administration of Civil and Criminal Law in the Colony, a Court

1893.

NOOR MOHAMED
v.
ALAMALOO.

of Requests for each Settlement. That Ordinance does not lay down any procedure; but, by section 54, retains the procedure then in force until otherwise provided by law. Section 81 gives Judges of the Supreme Court power to make all rules for the Court of Requests; but no rules have been made by the Judges, nor, so far as I know, does the Civil Procedure Ordinance deal with the Court of Requests*. The only other enactment that deals with the Court of Requests is section 10 of the Appeals Ordinance, of 1879. That section has been repealed to be re-enacted almost word for word by section 20 of the "Civil Appeals Ordinance, 1893." I have asked in vain for any enactment, Charter or Ordinance that gives power to the Court of Requests to order a new trial. The Acting Attorney-General admitted that he could not refer to any, but he suggested, that inasmuch as in the list of Court fees payable in respect of actions brought in the Court of Requests, there is an item of one dollar for the application of a new trial it may be assumed that the Court of Requests had the power to grant a re-hearing. But I do not agree with this. Such a power must be given expressly and cannot be implied. It is possible that there may have been such a rule prior to 1866; which in that year, may have been repealed and never re-enacted. And the item in the scale of fees may have been retained by inadvertence. However, that is a matter of mere speculation. It may be that the fee in question refers to an application of the following kind : Rule 4, of the Court of Requests Rules, of 1866, provides that, whether a defendant be present or not, the Court shall, upon due service of a copy of the summons upon the defendant, proceed to hear the matter contained in the summons. The Commissioner might be satisfied with the due service, and he might proceed with the matter; then the defendant might afterwards come and satisfy him that the summons had never been served upon him. In that case I think the Court would have jurisdiction to re-hear the action. It has been suggested that the Court of Requests has inherent jurisdiction to re-hear the case. No authority has been cited for this proposition, and, in the absence of authority, I am unable to concur with it. The Court of Requests cannot get jurisdiction by mere practice, but must have it conferred upon it by statutory authority. The jurisdiction of the High Court, in England, to re-hear a case was raised in the case of *Re St. Nazaire Co.*, (L. R. 12 C. D. 88;) and there it was deci-

* *Vide* Chap XXXVIII. sec. 437.

BONSER, C. J.
1893.
NOOR MOHAMED
v.
ALAMALOO.

ded that a Judge of the High Court had no power to re-hear an order made by himself or any other Judge, after the order has been drawn up. If I require any further support of the view I have formed. it seems to me I have it in section 10 of the Appeals Ordinance, of 1879. There it is assumed that you cannot have a re-hearing without an order from the Supreme Court. I am therefore of opinion that the Commissioner of the Court of Requests having heard and determined the matter in dispute, is *functus officio*.

Solicitors for the Apppellant.—*Khory and Brydges*.

THE QUEEN ON THE PROSECUTION OF CHARLES OTTO BLAGDEN. RESPONDENT.

v.

AKIM BIN JELOH, APPELLANT.

[MALACCA.]

Criminal Law—Section 188 of the Penal Code—Ordinance XII of 1872 sec. 46

There can be no conviction under section 188 of the Penal Code unless the order which the Defendant is charged with disobeying is couched in definite terms. A & B were adjoining land-owners. a cocoa-nut tree growing on A's land overhanging a house on B's land. C. a Magistrate and Justice of the Peace on the complaint of B who was afraid lest his house should be injured by falling cocoa-nuts, acting under sec. 46 of Ordinance XIII of 1872 made an order which was served on A which after reciting that it appeared to him (C) after due enquiry that a cocoa-nut tree belonging to the land of A overhanging the house of B in such a way as to be dangerous to life and property ordered A to cut down the said tree failing which B had authority to do so on tendering reasonable compensation to A.

A did not cut down the tree and it was subsequently cut down by the direction of C.

Held that A could not be convicted of an offence under sec. 188 of the Penal Code as the order was not couched in definite terms.

Semble C had no power to order A to cut down the cocoa-nut tree as the removal of the nuts would have been sufficient to prevent the injury apprehended.

BONSER, C. J.
1893.
Oct. 2.

THIS was an appeal from a conviction by Mr. Kyshe, Police Magistrate, Malacca, under section 188 of the Penal Code for that he the said Akim bin Jeloh did (knowingly) disobey an order promulgated by a public servant, to wit, the District Officer of Jasin. by refusing to cut down a cocoanut tree which was in his possession and was dangerous to life and injurious to the property of one Said bin Madris

On the 9th of August 1893, one Said bin Madris complained

BONSER, C. J. to Mr. Blagden the District Officer at Jasin that a cocoanut tree grow-
1893. ing upon the land of his neighbour (the Appellant) inclined over the
THE QUEEN ON complainant's house which was damaged by falling cocoanuts, and
THE
PROSECUTION desired that the Magistrate would order it to be cut down. Com-
OF
CHARLES OTTO plainant being willing to pay compensation.
BLAGDEN,
RESPONDENT.
v. The District Officer thereupon went to see the tree which was
AKIM BIN
JELOH, upon the land of the Appellant and came to the conclusion
APPELLANT.
that it was dangerous to human life and injurious to the property of
Complainant. The District Officer thereupon directed the Appellant
to appear before him and shew cause why the tree should not be cut
down, but advised the parties to settle the matter between themselves.
A few days subsequent to this the Appellant appeared before the District Officer and stated that he would not permit his cocoanut tree to
be cut down. On the 23rd August the Complainant again came to
the District Officer, and asked for an order that the tree should be cut
down, and believing it to an urgent case the District Officer thereupon
made an order as follows :—

On the Complaint of Said bin Madris.

Whereas it appears to the undersigned a Magistrate and Justice
of the Peace in and for the Settlement of Malacca after due enquiry that
a cocoanut tree belonging to the land of Akim bin Jeloh overhangs
the house of Said bin Madris in such a way as to be dangerous to life
and property.

This is to order the said Akim bin Jeloh to cut down the said
tree, failing which Said bin Madris has authority to do so on tendering reasonable compensation to Akim bin Jeloh.

(Sd.) C. Otto Blagden, 23rd August, 1893.

This order was served on the Appellant. Section 188 of the Penal
Code is as follows :—" Whoever, knowing that by an order promulga-
" ted by a public servant lawfully empowered to promulgate such order
" he is directed to abstain from a certain act, or to take certain order
" with certain property in his possession or under his management,
" disobeys such direction, shall, if such disobedience causes or tends
" to cause obstruction, annoyance, or injury, or risk of obstruction,
" annoyance or injury, to any persons lawfully employed, be punished
" with simple imprisonment for a term which may extend to one
" month, or with fine which may extend to one hundred dollars or
" with both and if such disobedience causes or tends to cause danger

" to human life, health, or safety or causes or tends to cause a riot
" or affray, shall be punished with imprisonment of either description
" for a term which may extend to six months or with fine which may
" extend to five hundred dollars, or with both."

BONSER, C. J.

1893.

THE QUEEN ON
THE
PROSECUTION
OF
CHARLES OTTO
BLAGDEN,
RESPONDENT,

v.

AKIM BIN
JELON,
APPELLANT.

On the 24th August, as the Appellant did not cut down the tree
the District Officer proceeded with some men to the neighbourhood
and in his presence the tree was cut down in spite of the protest of
the owner. The Appellant was subsequently charged with disobeying
an order promulgated by a public servant and was convicted and fined
$10.

The District Officer stated in his evidence before the Magistrate
that he had acted under Section 46 of Ordinance XIII of 1872 which is
as follows :—

" 1.—Any Magistrate, by a written order, may direct any person
" to abstain from a certain act, or to take certain order with certain
" property in his possession or under his management, whenever
" such Magistrate considers that such direction is likely to prevent
" or tends to prevent, obstruction, annoyance or injury, or risk of
" obstruction, annoyance, or injury, to any person lawfully employed ;
" or danger to human life, health, or safety ; or a riot or an affray.
" II—Such order may, in emergent cases or in cases where the cir-
" cumstances do not admit of the serving of notice, be passed exparte,
" and may in all cases be made upon such information as satisfies the
" Magistrate, and any Magistrate may recall or alter any order made
" under this section by him or by his predecessor in the same office."

Groom for the Appellant. Prosecutor states that the order
was made under Section 46 of the Criminal Procedure Ordinance XIII
of 1872. The wording of this section is the same as Section 62 of the
old Indian Code of Criminal Procedure (Act XXV of 1861)
corresponding with the Indian New Code of Criminal Procedure
(Act X of 1882). In such cases the Magistrate is empowered only
to direct any person " to abstain from any act " or to " take certain
order with certain property." It is submitted that " to take certain
order " does not empower the Magistrate to cut down and destroy the
private property of the Appellant. *Uttun Chunder Chatterjee v. Ram
Chunder Chatterjee* (5 Bengal Law Rep. 131). It may be that the
District Officer should have directed the Appellant to cut down his
nuts or in some way to prevent their falling on his neighbour's roof.

BONSER, C. J. but he could not utterly destroy and take away the Appellant's tree.

1893.

THE QUEEN ON THE PROSECUTION OF CHARLES OTTO BLAGDEN, RESPONDENT.

AKIM BIN JELOH, APPELLANT.

The section contained a wide and dangerous provision of the law and should be carefully watched lest it become an engine of oppresssion. Then the order was not "promulgated" as directed by the section and the District Officer is not "lawfully empowered" to promulgate it and the conviction omits to state that he was. To promulgate is not to send an order by hand to a private person; to promulgate is to publish publicly and in such manner as the local Government may direct.

But in any case the order is bad upon the face of it. It does not purport to have been issued under Ordinance XIII of 1872, or under any Ordinance at all and it does not appear that there is any penalty for disobedience. It does not bear the seal of any Court and there is no time specified in which the order if it be one, has to be carried out. There is no certainty about it. It is also in the alternative. It directs Appellant to cut down a tree "failing which Said bin Madris has authority to do so on tendering reasonable compensation to Akim bin Jeloh." It puts him to his election; he may do it or leave it alone. It cannot therefore be said that the Appellant was bound to obey any particular part of this order and it is impossible to say that he disobeyed it.

(He was stopped.)

Mr. Blagden in person being called upon by the Court to support the conviction cited Mayne's Commentaries [ed. 14 p. 169] "the validity "of an order is immaterial provided the order is promulgated by a "public servant who has power to make it." He had taken action as a Magistrate, not as a District Officer, and the conviction could be amended. The Jasin Court had no seal and the absence of a seal on this order could not be held to invalidate it. With regard to the promulgation of the order he cited Mayne p. 170. "Disobedience "to an order which has actually been brought to the knowledge of "the offender is punishable though the precise mode in which the "order ought to have been promulgated has not been followed" *re Parbulty* (6 Cal. 9). That in this case there had been promulgation, as the persons concerned had been informed of the order and if additional promulgation were required it was given by the Magistrate being present to see the order carried out. That the fact of the order being in the alternative made no difference. The second alternative might be mere surplusage and if so, it did not effect the validity of the rest of the order. If not, it was part of the order, and as such had been disobeyed. Acts included illegal omissions and *a fortiori* disobedience included active resistance to the second part of the order as well as non-performance of the first. The question of time was immaterial and did not render the order uncertain as it was evident on the fact of it that the Magistrate considered the matter one of urgency and therefore issued a peremptory order to take immediate effect. It was analogous in that respect to an *instanter* summons. The action could not be called " destruction of property " as full compensation had previously been offered; and even if it were, the property so destroyed was itself destroying that of the neighbour and the Respondent as a Magistrate took the only possible course to avoid further damage to the latter. As shewn in the evidence the tree in question had during the last few months begun to lean over towards the house and there was a danger of its eventually falling on it, though it is admitted that this was not the danger against which the order was primarily intended to guard.

BONSER, C. J.

1893.

THE QUEEN ON THE PROSECUTION OF CHARLES OTTO BLAGDEN.

v.

AKIM BIN JELOH, APPELLANT.

BONSER, C. J.

It seems to me this conviction cannot stand. When a man is convicted for breach of an order it should be couched in definite and unmistakeable terms. The order seems to be a direction to cut down a tree with an intimation that if he does not some one else may. A further point is whether the Magistrate had power to make such an order. I think the section was not intended to extend to cutting down a man's tree, because this is an irrevocable act. It seems to me that the section was intended to enable a Magistrate to abate a nuisance but not to give him power to make such an order as would necessitate the absolute destruction of property. The safety of the Complainant might have been secured by removing the fruit of the tree. I decide the case on the ground that the order is not such a definite one as that contemplated by Section 188 of the Penal Code. Of course if the tree were toppling to its fall there would be a danger of its falling on or crushing people, and it might be in the power of the Magistrate to have it secured by ropes or to have it cut down. In the present case there does not seem to me to have been any necessity for such an order and the conviction must be quashed.

> Conviction quashed and fine imposed ordered to be refunded.

Solicitor for the Appellant.—*S. R. Groom.*

R. M. S. VEERAPPA CHITTY.

v.

M. P. L. MOOTAPPA CHITTY.

[SINGAPORE.]

Foreign Judgment—Judgment in default of appearance against a Defendant who although served in the foreign country was neither resident in nor a subject of that country.

A judgment of a foreign Court obtained in default of appearance against a Defendant cannot be enforced by action in the Courts of this Colony where the Defendant although served with the writ of summons whilst temporarily present in the foreign country on business, was not a subject of nor resident in such foreign country for there exists nothing imposing on the Defendant any duty to obey the judgment. *Kader Nina Marican v. Kader Meydin* (S. S. L. R. [1893] 4) distinguished.

Quaere, whether a judgment of the Supreme Court of Johore will be enforced by the Courts of this Colony.

BONSER, C. J.
————
1893.
Oct. 10 & 17.

THIS was an action on a judgment obtained by the Plaintiff against the Defendant in the Supreme Court of Johore.

Donaldson & Napier, for the Plaintiff.

Nanson & Delay, for the Defendant.

The facts and the arguments are sufficiently set forth in the judgment. In addition to the cases noticed in the judgment the following cases were cited; *Buchanan v. Rucker* (1 Camp 63); The *Delta* (L. R. 1 P. D. 393); *Jackson v. Spittall* (L. R. 5. C. P. 542); *General Steam Navigation Co., v. Guillon* (1 M. & W. 894).

C. A. V.

BONSER, C. J.

This is an action brought upon a judgment of the Court of Johore for $20,000. The Defendant is a British Indian subject residing in Singapore. The proceedings in the Johore Court were commenced on the 6th March 1893 by the issue of a summons in the Malay language by the Johore Commissioner of Police, requiring the Defendant to attend with his books and papers at the Police Court, which is the only Court in Johore, and where all cases, civil and criminal alike, are tried. The summons was served on the Defendant in Johore, whither he had gone for the day on business. The Defendant is not a Johore subject nor has he ever resided there nor was he present in Johore when the summons was issued.

BONSER, C. J.

1893.

R. M. S. VEE-
KAPPA CHITTY.
v.
M P. L. MOO-
TAPPA CHITTY.

The Defendant did not appear on the summons, either personally or by agent, and on the 25th of March judgment was given against him in his absence for the full amount claimed. Upon that judgment this action is brought. The Defendant raises (amongst other defences) the defence that a judgment thus obtained in his absence imposes no duty on him to obey it. The Plaintiff on the other hand contends that the fact that the Defendant was served with the summons during his temporary presence in Johore constrains this Court to enforce the judgment. The question is one of considerable importance to the mercantile community of this Settlement, for if the contention of the Plaintiff be correct, every merchant who spends a Sunday in Johore renders himself liable to have his business rights and obligations adjudicated upon by a Mohammedan judge administering Mohammedan law.

The cases in which English Courts will enforce the judgments of foreign Courts obtained against British subjects and others in their absence are enumerated by Fry, J. in *Rousillon v. Rousillon.* (14 Ch. D. p. 371), in the following words :—

" What are the circumstances which have been held to impose upon the defendant the duty of obeying the decision of a foreign Court? Having regard to the case of *'chilsby v. Westenholz* (L. R. 6 Q. B. 155) and to *Copin v. Adamson* (L. R. 9 Exch. 345) they may, I think, be stated thus. The Courts of this country consider the defendant bound where he is a subject of a foreign country in which the judgment has been obtained ; where he was a resident in the foreign country when the action began : where the defendant in the character of plaintiff has selected the forum in which he is afterward sued: where he has voluntarily appeared; where he has contracted to submit himself to the forum in which the judgment was obtained; and possibly, if *Becquet v. MacCarthy* (3 B. & A. 951) be right, where the defendant has real estate within the foreign jurisdiction, in respect of which the cause of action arose whilst he was within that jurisdiction."

It would seem therefore that in order to impose on a defendant the obligation of fulfilling a foreign judgment obtained against him in his absence, the defendant must either be a subject of the foreign

BONSER, C. J.

1893.

R. M. S VEE-
RAPPA CHITTY.
v.
M. P. L. MOO-
TAPPA CHITTY.

state or have so conducted himself as to warrant the inference that he has or ought to have submitted himself to the jurisdiction of the Courts. For instance, if he is domiciled or, short of being domiciled, is a more or less permanent resident in the foreign state, he will be taken to owe submission to the jurisdiction of the Court in return for the protection which he enjoys, or as it has been expressed. he owes a qualified or temporary allegiance to that country.   Another example is where the plaintiff has elected to sue in the foreign court and perhaps where, as defendant. he has voluntarily appeared before the foreign court and taken the chance of a judgment in his favour.   Now can it be inferred from the fact that a man goes to Johore for the day that he intends to submit himself to the jurisdiction of the Johore Court ? To my mind such an inference would be in the highest degree unreasonable. Then is there anything unconscientious in this Defendant saying to the Plaintiff, 'If you have a claim against me I desire to have it decided in the Court of this Colony where we both reside and carry on business, and I decline to obey the judgments of the Johore Court ?' In my opinion there is not.   I can see nothing in the circumstances of this case nor in the conduct of the Defendant. which leads me to the conclusion that the Defendant has in fact submitted to the jurisdiction or that he ought to have done so.   But whether or not the principle which I have suggested be the true one, the fact remains that no case can be found in which an English Court has enforced a foreign judgment against a British subject obtained under circumstances like the present. A case, however, of *Kader Nina Merican v. Kader Meydin*, (S. S. L. R., [1893], p 4,) has been cited, which was decided in this Court by Sidgreaves, C, J., as far back as 1876 but only reported this year, and by which it is said I am bound.   Sir Thomas Sidgreaves in giving judgment said :—

  " It was next objected that the Court of Johore had no jurisdiction to try this case inasmuch as the defendant was not resident in and had no property in Johore. The defendant himself however according to his own account went to Johore for the express purpose of opposing the present plaintiff and according to the plaintiff when he applied for a warrant in the first instance against the defendant. the defendant appeared in Court to oppose the application and was so far successful that the warrant was refused and only a summons issued against him. The objection to the jurisdiction of the Court

BONSER, C. J.

1893.

R. M. N. VEE-
RAPPA CHITTY.
v.
M. P. L. MEO-
TAPPA CHITTY.

hardly comes with a good grace from him. I have no hesitation in deciding however that the Johore Court had jurisdiction to try the case and that the temporary presence of of the defendant in Johore was sufficient to give the Court jurisdiction. Actions are either local or transitory and the present action was of the latter class. *Debitum et contractus sunt nullius loci* and it is upon this principle that actions are constantly tried in the Courts here."

It might be sufficient to say that there were facts in that case which do not exist in the present. from which it might be inferred that the defendant had submitted himself to the jurisdiction of the Johore Court, but the learned Judge clearly rests his decision on the ground that inasmuch as this Court asserts jurisdiction over defendants who are temporarily present, so it will recognise the right of foreign courts to do the same. But this ground was expressly repudiated by the Court of Queen's Bench in *Godard v. Gray*. (L. R. 6 Q. B., 139,) and *Schibsby v. Westonholz*, (L. R. 6 Q. B. 155,) in which latter case Blackburn, J., says, delivering the judgment of the Court :—

" We are much pressed on the argument with the fact that the British Legislature has by the Common Law Procedure Act 1852 (15 and 16 Vic. c. 76 ss. 18 and 19) conferred on our Courts a power of summoning foreigners under certain circumstances to appear and in case they do not, giving judgment against them by default. It was this consideration principally which induced me at the trial to entertain the opinion which I then expressed and have since changed. And we think that if the principle on which foreign judgments were enforced was that which is loosely called 'comity' we could hardly decline to enforce a foreign judgment given in France against a resident of Great Britain under circumstances hardly if at all distinguishable from those under which we, *mutatis mutandis*, might give judgment against a resident in France: but it is quite different if the principle be that which we have just laid down."

The decision of Sidgreaves, C. J. therefore, unless it can supported on the grounds which I have suggested, is inconsistent with the decisions of the Court of Queen's Bench in *Godard v. Gray* (L. R. 6 Q. B. 139) and *Schibsby v. Westonholz*, (L. R. 6 Q. B. 155) and, also with the subsequent decision of the Court of Exchequer in *Copin v. Adamson*. (L. R. 9 Exch. 345) which followed and adopted these decisions ; and is not binding on me. It may be remarked that none of these cases

BONSER, C. J. appear to have been cited before the late Chief Justice.

Another objection was raised by the Defendant that the Court in Johore was not a Court whose judgment could be recognised by this Court. It appears that in the Court of Johore the law is Mohammedan law administered by a native Mohammedan Judge. That law was stated by the Johore lawyer who was called for the Plaintiff to be the law of the Koran supplemented by the edicts or ordinances of the Ruler, but he added that any such edict or ordinance, unless in accordance with the law of the Koran, was *ipso facto* void. So far as I am aware there is no case except the one above referred to, of *Kadir Nina Merican v. Kadir Meydin* (S. S L. R. [1893] 3) in which an English Court has recognised the judgment of a Mohammedan Court as binding on British subjects. This may be accounted for by the fact that in the great majority of Mohammedan, and indeed Oriental countries, the subjects of European Powers are exempted by treaty from the jurisdiction of the local Court and can only be sued in Courts of their own nationality.

The rules of private international law are rules which have been evolved from the law and practice of the Courts of the great family of European nations and are primarily intended to govern the relations *inter se* of the members of that family. I doubt whether the State of Johore is yet in a position to assert its title to be received into that family and successfully insist that this Court shall accord to the judgments of its Courts an effect and force which are not accorded to the judgments of the Courts of the Kingdoms of Persia and Siam, and of the Empires of Turkey, China and Japan. But it is not necessary in the view which I take of this case to decide that point. At the same time I wish carefully to guard myself against its being supposed that I entertain any doubts as to the good faith of the Johore Court or its competence or ability to decide questions arising between Johore subjects, and that I desire to speak in any terms but those of the greatest respect of that Court. It was indeed alleged by the Defendant that the judgment in the present case was contrary to natural justice, but there was nothing in the evidence to support that allegation and I do not believe that there was any foundation for it.

With regard to the costs of the action the Defendant has placed on the record a charge of fraud which he has not attempted to substantiate. This being so I shall not give him any costs. But he has further disputed the fact that the summons was served on him in

Johore and has sworn that the service took place in Singapore and has brought witnesses to swear the same thing. I do not believe him or his witnesses and I regret that I cannot make him pay the costs of the action. I can however make him pay the costs of the issue as to the place of service, and I do so.

BONSER, C. J.

1893.

R. M. S. VEE-RAPPA CHITTY.

M. P. L. MOO-TAPPA CHITTY.

Judgment will be for the Defendant, without costs, and the Defendant must pay to the Plaintiff the costs I have mentioned.

Solicitors for the Plaintiff—*Drew & Napier*.

Solicitors for the Defendant—*S. R. Groom*.

MOHAMED MEYDIN *v.* SYED AHMED.

[SINGAPORE.]

Statute of Limitations.—Clause 9 of Indian Act XIV of 1859.—Amendment at trial.

The Plaintiff sued the Defendant to recover a sum of money paid by him in satisfaction of a judgment obtained against him and the Defendant upon their joint and several promissory note which the Plaintiff had signed as surety for the Defendant.

The judgment was obtained in 1886. The judgment debt was paid by the Plaintiff in March 1889 and the present action was not commenced till September 1893. The Defendant contended that the period of limitation was that provided by clause 9 of Indian Act XIV of 1859 namely 3 years and the claim was therefore barred.

Held that clause 9 was not intended to apply to a claim framed in accordance with the *common indebitatus* counts for money had and received except in the cases mentioned in the clause namely " for money lent " or " for interest " and that the following words " for the breach of any contract " do not include an action brought upon an implied contract and that consequently there being no express provision for the case it fell under Clause 16.

Radhanath Dutt v. Govind Chunder Chatterjee (4 W.R.S.C. 19) followed.

THIS was a Small Cause in which the Plaintiffs' claim as endorsed on the writ was as follows :—

BONSER, C. J.

1893.
Oct. 20, 27 & 30.

$442,26 for money paid to P.P.L. Raman Chitty as surety for the Defendant, being the amount of a judgment dated 9th September 1886 obtained by the said Raman Chitty against the Plaintiff and Defendant in an action on a promissory note.

The Defence filed was a plea of payment and satisfaction but at the trial Counsel applied for leave to amend by pleading the Statute of Limitations which was granted.

The facts of the case sufficiently appear in the judgment.

T. de M. Braddell who appeared for the Plaintiff contended on the authorities of

Doorga Doss v Doorga Monee Dossee.—(2 W. R. 216.)

Nobokieto Bhunj v Rajbullubh Bhunj.—(3 W. R. 134.)

Radhanath Dutt v Govind Chunder Chatterjee.—(4 W. R. S. C. 19.)
that the provisions of clause 9 of the Statute did not apply to an action like the present where the Plaintiff sued for an ascertained amount and not for damages for a breach of contract. The words "any contract" meant any "express" contract and were not intended to include "implied" contracts as was to be gathered from reading the latter part of the clause which excepted written contracts. Where the contract had to be implied there could be no question of its being in writing. The clause did not expressly provide for the present case and consequently the provisions of clause 16 governed the limitation to be applied.

Buckley, for the Defendant, contended that the words "any contract" were intended to cover all contracts whether express or implied. He referred to the cases of *Tripp v. Kubeer Mundel* (9 Suth. W. R. 209) and *Parushnath Misser v. Shaik Bundar Ali* (6 W. R. 132.)

BONSER, C. J.

This is a matter of considerable difficulty owing to conflicting decisions of the Indian Courts upon the meaning of the words "breach of any contract" in clause 9 of sec. 1 of Indian Act XIV of 1859. Under these circumstances I have to decide what is the correct interpretation of those words. The Plaintiff and Defendant were joint makers of a promissory note to a Chitty. Plaintiff was surety for the Defendant. The promissory note was not met by the Defendant when it became due and the holder thereof sued the Plaintiff and Defendant and the Plaintiff had to pay the amount due under the judgment.

The claim in the present action is framed in accordance with the count for "money paid" which is one of the counts which were known as the "*common indebitatus* counts" that is, the Plaintiff sues as he is clearly entitled to do for a sum certain as being money paid by him at the Defendant's request. It would have also been open to him to sue upon a special count and claim unliquidated damages for the breach of the contract of indemnity which was implied from the nature of the transaction. The question which I have to decide is whether this action brought in this form is an action brought for the breach of a contract within the meaning of clause 9 of Indian Act XIV of 1859.

It will be observed that the scheme of the Indian Act is to enumerate
a number of cases applying the appropriate period of limitation to each
and finally to provide in a general clause for " all suits for which no
other limitation is hereby expressly provided."

Of the eight forms of *common indebitatus* counts, two are specified in
clause 9 namely those for " money lent " and " interest " and those are
followed by the words " or for the breach of any contract."

It is contended by the Defendant that the words " or for the breach
of any contract " cover every case in which an action is based upon a contract whether express or implied ; in other words that they are a general description which includes the two instances of actions brought for
" money lent " and actions brought for " interest " immediately before
specified. The Plaintiff contends that they define a distinct class of
actions which does include the present.

If the Defendant's contention is right, the Plaintiff's action is
barred, being brought more than 3 years after the cause of action ac-
crued. So far as I know there are no decisions on the point in this
Court.

The Indian decisions are conflicting.

It has been held in *Doyle v. Allum Biswas.* (4 W.R.S.C. 1,) that
the limitation in an action on an ' account stated ' which is one of the
common indebitatus counts is 3 years because it was an action for the
breach of a contract. On the other hand it was held in *Radhanath
Dutt v. Govind Chunder Chatterjee*(4 W. R. S. C. 19) being an action
for " money had and received " that the period of limitation is 6 years
because the Act has no express provision for that case.

Again it has been held that the period of limitation for an action
for the price of goods sold and delivered is 3 years on the ground that
it was an action " upon a contract," but the words of the clause are
not " actions upon any contract " but " actions for the breach of any
contract." I think that the difference of phraseology is material. All
the actions on the *common indebitatus* counts are in a sense " actions
upon contracts " inasmuch as the debt sued for arises out of a contract
either express or implied, but they could not properly be styled
" actions for the breach of contract." The description would in my
opinion more correctly apply to actions on special counts where unliquidated damages are claimed.

BONSER, C. J.

1893.

MOHAMED
MEYDIN
v.
SYED AHMED.

I have come to the conclusion, though not without much hesitation, that what the legislature has done is this. It has selected actions on two of the most commonly used of the *common indebitatus* counts for special limitation and has not made any express provision for the others, which will consequently fall under clause 16 of the Act. It has also made special provision for actions brought on what would have been formerly called special counts in actions on contracts where unliquidated damages are claimed, for this is what I understand by the words " actions for the breach of any contract."

This present action I hold not to be an action within the meaning of those words. It is therefore not expressly provided for and the period of limitation is 6 years.

It was also argued by Mr. Braddell that even if the action had been brought in the form of an action for unliquidated damages for the breach of the implied contract of indemnity, the result would be the same, for that the word " contract " means " express contract " and does not include " implied contract." There appears to be an Indian decision to this effect, but I venture to doubt whether this is a correct interpretation of the clause and I prefer to rest my decision on the other ground.

I decide this question in favour of the Plaintiff most reluctantly for in my opinion the law of limitation of actions is a most beneficial law and I am extremely unwilling to do anything to restrict its scope.

The Indian Act XIV of 1859 has long since been repealed in India and replaced by a more complete and intelligible enactment and it is high time that this Colony followed the example.

Solicitors for the Plaintiff—*Braddell Brothers & Matthews.*
Solicitors for the Defendant—*Rodyk & Davidson.*

LEE AH TOKE

v.

CHAN AH FAT AND CHAN AH LYE.

[SINGAPORE.]

Landlord & Tenant—Tenant holding over after expiration of term.

Where a tenant held for a term of years and after the expiration of the lease continued in possession of the premises, paying rent for his holding, *Held* that he was a monthly tenant, the custom of the colony being to hold houses on monthly tenancies, and that a month's notice to quit was sufficient to determine his tenancy.

Syed Mohamed Alsagoff v. Max Behr (1. Kyshe 637,) distinguished.

GATTY, J.

1893.

July 12 & 13
&
Oct. 3.

THIS was an action to recover possession of four houses, No. 215 South Bridge Road, and Nos. 24, 25, and 26 North Canal Road.

The Plaintiff by his statement of claim alleged that on the 3rd of October, 1892, the date of the dissolution of a certain partnership carried on at the said premises and known as Chop Syn Yin Nam, in which the Defendant Chan Ah Lye, and other persons were partners, the said Chop and subsequently to the dissolution thereof, the persons forming the partnership therein held the said premises as monthly tenants of one Leonard Johannes Scheerder, that by an indenture dated the 20th of December, 1892, Scheerder demised the said premises to the Plaintiff for the term of five years, from the 1st of January 1893; that the tenancy of the persons forming the partnership known as Syn Yin Nam was duly determined by notice to quit expiring on the 28th of February, 1893; and that the Defendants were in possession of the said premises.

The action was discontinued as against the Defendant, Chan Ah Fat, he denying that he had ever been in possession of the property in dispute. The Defendant, Chan Ah Lye, pleaded possession.

At the trial it appeared that the question between the parties was whether the premises in question were held on a monthly tenancy, as alleged by the Plaintiff, or on a yearly tenancy as alleged by the Defendant, Chan Ah Lye. It appeared from Scheerder's evidence, and his books, that he had managed the property as attorney or as trustee since 1885, and that the receipts for rent had been sometimes made out in the name of the Chop Syn Yin Nam, and sometimes in the names of individual partners, but since May, 1890, and until January 1893, they had always been made in the name of the firm. The rent had been gradually raised from time to time. Evidence was also given on behalf of the Plaintiff that monthly tenancies were the usual tenancies in Singapore.

The Defendant, Chan Ah Lye, produced in evidence a Lease of the 25th February 1885, whereby one W. G. Cunningham, the then owner of the property, by his attorney, Scheerder, demised No. 215 South Bridge Road, and No. 24 North Canal Road to the Defendant, Chan Ah Lye, described as of the Chop Syn Yin Nam, for the term of 3 years from the 1st day of January, 1885, at the rental of $36 per month. The Defendant Chan Ah Lye, proved that, subsequent to this Lease, the Chop rented from Mr. Cunningham Nos. 25 and 26 North

GATTY, J.   Canal Road, which adjoined the property comprised in the Lease, and
1893.   the whole block was used by the Chop as an eating-house. On the
Lee Ah Toke   expiration of the Lease of the 25th February, 1835, the Defendant alleged
v.
Chan Ah Fat   that it was agreed, that he should continue to hold the premises con-
and
Chan Ah Lye.   tained in the Lease under the terms of the lease and not as a monthly
tenant, and that all the repairs required had been done at the cost of
the Chop Syn Yin Nam.

Napier for the Plaintiff.

T. de M. Braddell for the Defendant, Chan Ah Lye.

Where a tenant holds for a term of years and, after the expiration of the lease, continues in possession, paying rent, the presumption of law is that he is a tenant from year to year, and at least 6
months notice is required to determine such tenancy. *Syed Mohamed
Alsagoff v. Max Behr*, (1, Kyshe 637,) *Dougal* v. *Mc. Carthy* (L. R.
[1893] 1. Q. B. 736.)

Mere raising of rent is not sufficient to rebut the presumption;
Doe d Monck v. Geekie (5 Q. B. 841.) He also cited *Digby v. Atkinson*
(4 Camp., 178) ; *Hyatt v. Griffiths*, (17 Q. B. 508,) *John v. Jenkins* (1 C
& M, 227.)

Napier, The question is one of fact to be determined by the
circumstances of the case. The circumstances of the Colony where
monthly tenancies are the invariable rule are quite different from those
of England. He cited the notes to *Richardson v. Langridge*, Tudor's
Leading Cases in Real Property. p. 4.

Cur. adv. vult.

GATTY, J.

(After reading the pleadings, continued.) As to two of these
houses, Nos. 25 and 26 North Canal Road, the evidence was that they
had been taken by the firm and the Defendant had not been in possession of any agreement in writing with the Plaintiff for the tenancy
of these houses. Therefore I hold that as to these houses the notice
that has been given is sufficient, and that the Plaintiff is entitled to
recover possession. As to houses Nos. 215 South Bridge Road, and
24 North Canal Road, the defence set up was that the Defendant was
a yearly tenant. A substantial question was raised; firstly whether in
law such a yearly tenancy had been created, and secondly, what notice
to quit was required. Had this case been before me in England I think I
should have decided it by the Common Law, which requires six months'

notice to quit on either side. But I am deciding the case in the Colony of the Straits Settlements, and no authority has been cited to me to shew what the law on such a point as this is in the Colony. There are some things to which it is applied; but I think that the Common Law on such a point as this is excluded, and what is to guide the Court in coming to a conclusion on such matters as this is the provision in the Charter, of 1855 (page 18, Volume I, Harwood's Ordinances,)which says that Judges are "to pass judgment and sentence according to justice and right." Again by section 6, of the Civil Law Ordinance, of 1878, I find that, though the Mercantile Law of England is expressly imported, there is a proviso that nothing herein contained shall be taken to introduce into this Colony any part of the law of England relating to the tenure, or conveyance, or assurance of, or succession to, any land or other immoveable property, or any estate, right, or interest therein. What am I to be guided by ? The Common Law of England is a good guide, if it is applicable; but I think I should be acting contrary to my conscience if I were to hold, that either of these parties, if there was an implied contract, had any idea at all in their minds after the tenancy expired that there was going to arise a tenancy from year to year in which 6 months' notice to quit was necessary. There is some evidence as to what took place at the expiration of the Lease. Scheerder says that it was to be a monthly tenancy. The Defendant said that he went to Scheerder, asked him what was going to happen, and applied for a new lease; and that Scheerder refused to give him a new lease ; but said he could go on the same terms as under the old lease. That is hardly enough to constitute a complete contract of tenancy because he had to supply the term which was to be implied from the circumstances of the case. I think that what I ought to do is to put such a term into the contract as my judgment dictates may be fairly considered to have been in the minds of both parties. I believe that the contract which might fairly be considered to be in the minds of both parties was a monthly tenancy, because I think it is practically the custom of the country, and that it is not the custom of the country to enter into yearly contracts requiring six months' notice. I have read the case of *Syed Mohamed Alsagoff v. Max Behr* (1 Kyshe 637) and of course I do not say that Sir Theodore Ford was wrong in his judgment of that particular case. I find that the law, as laid down in England now, is, that this is rather a question of evidence, a question of what the im-

GATTY, J.

1893.

LEE AH TORE
v.
CHAN AH FAT
AND
CHAN AH LYE.

GATTY, J.
1893.
LEE AH TOKE
v.
CHAN AH FAT
AND
CHAN AH LYE.

plied contract was.   I think it would be a most serious decision for me to come to, that these people, accustomed to a monthly tenancy should be saddled with a yearly tenancy, subject to six months' notice to quit, when it was not the least in their minds when the contract was entered into.   I think that so far as the Common Law can be followed it should be followed.   In England, the notice required followed the custom, therefore, I think that here the usual notice, a month's notice is sufficient.   I therefore hold that a proper notice to quit according to the law of this Colony has been given as to premises Nos. 24 North Canal Road and 215 South Bridge Road, and therefore the Plaintiff is entitled to recover possession of the premises.

Judgment for the Plaintiff with costs.

Solicitors for the Plaintiff.—*Drew & Napier.*

Solicitors for the Defendant, Chan Ah Lye,—*Braddell Brothers and Matthews.*

CHOP BAN GUAN LEONG.

v.

QUAIK KONG AND OTHERS.

[SINGAPORE.]

Practice—Costs—Taxation of successful pauper defendant—Civil Procedure Ordinance 1878 sec. 461—Ordinance XVII of 1886 sec. 2 (3.)

A successful plaintiff in an action in formâ pauperis is entitled upon taxation as against the defendant only to his solicitor's costs out of pocket together with a reasonable allowance to cover office expenses, &c., and cannot be allowed anything for remuneration to his solicitor or fees to counsel.

COX, C. J.
1893.
Nov. 20.

AFTER the commencement of this action the Defendant Quaik Kong obtained leave to defend in formâ pauperis and judgment was given in his favour with costs.   The Defendant's Solicitors sent in a bill of costs amounting to $248.20 in which they claimed the scale charges, and the Plaintiffs objected to the Defendant being allowed more than out of pocket costs and a reasonable allowance to cover office expenses &c.   *C. B. Buckley* for the Plaintiffs cited *Carson v Pickersgill.* (L. R. 14 Q. B. D. 859); and *Johnson v. Lindsay* (L. R. [1892] A. C. 110).   The Registrar on taxation merely allowed the Defendant $11.40 i.e. costs out of pocket &c. and the Defendant being

COX, C. J.

1893.

CHOP BAN
QUAN LEONG
v.
QUAIK KONG
AND OTHERS.

dissatisfied, applied under Order III r. 24 of the Costs Rules for a review of the taxation. The matter came before Cox C. J. on the 29th November 1893.

T. de M. Braddell for the Defendant contended that the cases relied on by the Plaintiffs were decisions on the English rules which were not in force here and that the wording of sec. 461 of the Civil Procedure Ordinance of 1878 entitled the successful pauper's Advocate & Solicitor to the same fees and remuneration as he would be entitled to, if the Defendant had not obtained leave to defend as a pauper, and that the reasons for not allowing the successful pauper *dives costs* in England, did not apply to this Colony.

Buckley for the Plaintiffs. The pauper has Counsel and Solicitor assigned him by the Court, he pays them nothing, therefore he can recover nothing as it would go into his pocket. The services are given to the pauper and not to his adversary.

COX, C. J.

This is an application made to me in Chambers for the revision of a decision of the Registrar upon the taxation of Defendant's costs in the above case. The Defendant Quaik Kong who had defended the action in formâ pauperis, an Advocate & Solicitor having been assigned to him by the Court, obtained judgment with costs against the Plaintiffs. In the Bill of Costs submitted for taxation, fees for the remuneration of the Advocate and Solicitor were charged; but the Registrar disallowed those charges being of opinion that only fees out of pocket and an allowance to cover office expenses should be sanctioned. For the Defendant it was contended before me that the decision of the Registrar is contrary to section 461 of the Civil Procedure Ordinance which provides that when a suitor in formâ pauperis succeeds and costs are awarded against his opponent then the Advocate & Solicitor assigned shall be entitled to and shall receive all such fees as the Registrar shall allow him on taxation. The Plaintiffs quoted in support of the view taken by the Registrar, *Carson v. Pickersgill* (L. R. 14 Q. B. D. 859) and *Johnson v. Lindsay* (L. R. [1892] A. C. 110.)

Before the decision in *Carson v. Pickersgill* referred to above, much uncertainty existed in the Courts in England as to what costs should be awarded to a pauper litigant who had been successful. In Chancery the pauper was allowed *dives costs* (i. e, costs as other suitors) on the ground laid down by Lord Somers (quoted by Bowen

COX, C. J.
1893.
CHOP BAN
GUAN LEONG
v.
QUAIK KONG
AND OTHERS.

L. J. in *Carson v Pickersgill*) that "though he was at no costs yet the counsel and clerks do not give their labour to the defendant but to the pauper." In the Common Law Courts the practice appears to have been that when a pauper recovered more than £ 5 he was considered as "dispaupered" the effect of his being dispaupered being that he was enabled to pay his Counsel and Solicitor and recover the amount from the opposite side. The practice was however disapproved in *Dooly v Great Northern Railway Co.* (4 E & B 341.) In *Carson v Pickersgill* (L. R. 14 Q. B. D. 859) it was held by the Court of Appeal (affirming the decision of the Queen's Bench Division) that the pauper is entitled upon taxation as against his opponent only to costs out of pocket and cannot be allowed anything for remuneration to his Solicitor or fees to Counsel. The decision rests upon very plain ground, costs are given to a successful litigant to compensate him for the expenses he has had to incur, or which he may have rendered himself liable to pay; now a pauper has not to pay and he is not liable to pay any fees to his Counsel and Solicitor who are prohibited from taking any remuneration from him and therefore he cannot recover from his opponent what he has not paid or is not liable to pay. The principles thus laid down were acted upon by the House of Lords in *Johnson v. Lindsay* (L. R. [1892,] A. C. 110): There, a pauper having been successful on his appeal, the officer of the House in taxing the costs allowed fees to Counsel and Solicitor's costs and charges. But it was held that fees to Counsel should be disallowed and that the Solicitor should have only his costs out of pocket with a reasonable allowance to cover office expenses including clerks &c. The law in England is thus well settled, but it was urged that a different rule must prevail in this Colony as section 461 of the Civil Procedure Ordinance recognises that the Advocate & Solicitor assigned to a pauper litigant should receive fees to be allowed by the Registrar on taxation. This provision taken by itself would certainly make it difficult to follow the principles laid down in the cases quoted above. But I think it must be read with section 2(3) of Ordinance XVII of 1886 which provides that taxation of costs shall be governed by and conducted upon the law and principles by and upon which the taxation of costs is for the time being governed and conducted in the Supreme Court of Judicature in England. The Registrar was therefore bound to follow the

decisions quoted above in taxing the costs in this cause and in confor-
mity with these decisions he was right in refusing to allow the fees to
the Advocate & Solicitor, except costs out of pocket and a reasonable
allowance to cover office expenses including clerks &c.

I must therefore uphold his decision and dismiss this Summons.
No costs on this application.

Solicitors for the Plaintiffs.—*Rodyk & Davidson.*
Solicitors for the Defendant.—*Braddell Brothers & Matthews.*

COX, C. J.

1893.

CHOP BAN
GUAN LEONG
v
QUAIE KONG
AND OTHERS.

HAJI HASMAH BINTE MOHAMED SEEDA MALIM

v.

HAJI ASHIM BIN MOHAMED IRSALAY.

[SINGAPORE.]

Practice—Stamps—Cancellation—Ordinance II of 1881 Sec. 9.

If at the time an adhesive stamp is affixed to an document chargeable with
duty, such document has not been executed by any person, it is not necessary
that the stamp should be cancelled in the manner provided by sec. 9 of Ordinance II of 1881.

DURING the progress of this case *Donaldson* (who with *Fort*
appeared on behalf of the Defendant), tendered as evidence a
document purporting to be a receipt signed by the Plaintiff. *Drew*
(with him *Delay*) on behalf of the Plaintiff objected to this being
admitted as evidence on the ground that though there was a receipt
stamp on it the stamp was not cancelled according to the terms of
section 9, of Ordinance II, of 1881. *Drew* submitted that this section
required that the stamp should be cancelled by writing or marking
distinctly the date in ink either wholly on the stamp or partly on the
stamp and partly on the paper, and that, as in this case this had not
been done, by section 9, sub-section 2, the document was not duly

COX., C. J.

1893.
Dec. 19.

COX, C. J. stamped, and therefore by section 32 was not admissible in evidence.

1893. Sub-sections 1 and 2, of section 9, are as follows :—

HAJI HASMAH
BINTE
MOHAMED
SERDA MALIM
v.
HAJI ARNIS
BIN MOHAMED
IRSALAY.

> I. Whoever affixes any adhesive stamp to any instrument chargeable with duty and which has been executed by any person, shall, when affixing such stamp, cancel the same, by writing or marking distinctly the date in ink, either wholly on the stamp, or partly on the stamp and partly on the paper on which the stamp is affixed, or in such other manner as the Governor in Council may, from time to time, direct, so that the stamp cannot be used again; and whoever executes any instrument on any paper bearing an adhesive stamp shall, at the time of execution, unless such stamp has been already cancelled in manner aforesaid, cancel the same in manner aforesaid, so that it cannot be used again.
>
> II. Any instrument bearing an adhesive stamp which has not been so cancelled so that it cannot be used again shall, so far as such stamp is concerned, be deemed to be unstamped,

Donaldson pointed out that, at the time the adhesive stamp had been put on the document, no person had executed the document, and that, therefore, section 9, did not apply and that sub-section 2 did not require that the stamp should be cancelled in any particular way, but submitted that " so cancelled so that it cannot be used again " merely meant to be cancelled in any way so that it could not be used, and did not require to be cancelled in a particular way as described by sub-section 1.

COX, C. J.

I do not think the second point arises in this case, so that it is not necessary for me to determine whether " cancelled so that it cannot be used again " means cancelled in the way described in the first sub-section or not. But I do not think that sub-section 1 applies to this case as the document on which the receipt stamp was affixed had not been executed at the time the receipt stamp was affixed.

Solicitor for the Plaintiff.—*S. R. Groom.*

Solicitors for the Defendant.—*Donaldson & Burkinshaw.*

IN THE MATTER OF ONG HONG NEO, AN INFANT.

[SINGAPORE.]

Practice—Habeas Corpus—Indian Act IX of 1861.

The proper mode of proceeding to obtain the custody of an infant is by petition under Indian Act IX of 1861, and not by writ of Habeas Corpus.

THIS was a motion by Ong Yong Beng for a rule nisi for a writ of Habeas Corpus against Lee Quee Neo the mother of the infant who had taken the infant out of the possession of Ong Yong Beng who had had the custody of the infant for the last two years under an adoption agreement to which the mother was a party.

Brydges for the Applicant.

COX, C. J.

Referred to the Indian Act IX of 1861 and said that applications of this nature should be made under that Act by petition. and directed that a petition should be filed, and made an order for the production of the infant as upon the petition.

Solicitors for the Applicant.—*Khory & Brydges.*

COX, C. J.

1894.
Feb. 21.

TAN MEE NEO

v.

TAN TUG

[SINGAPORE.]

Support—Implied Grant.

In January 1878, the Plaintiff's predecessor in title conveyed a plot of land to the Defendant's predecessor in title retaining the land adjoining it on one side, the Defendant's predecessor in title having notice that the Plaintiff's predecessor in title intended to use such adjoining land for building purposes. In May 1878, the Plaintiff's predecessor in title conveyed such adjoining land to the Plaintiff who subsequently erected two houses on it one of which was on the extreme edge of the land where it adjoined the Defendant's land. In June 1893, the Defendant dug a trench on the edge of his land flush with the wall and foundations of one of the Defendant's houses, in order to lay the foundations of a house. A very heavy shower of rain coming down. the trench filled with water and the Plaintiff's house fell down.

Held that the Plaintiff had no cause of action against the Defendant.

Semble where land is conveyed to a purchaser the vendor retaining other land upon which to the knowledge of the purchaser he intends to build, there is no implied grant on the part of the purchaser of a right of support to any houses which the vendor may thereafter build on the land retained by him.

BONSER, C. J.
1893.
Nov. 1.

THE facts of the case sufficiently appear from the judgment.

Donaldson appeared for the Plaintiff.

Joaquim appeared for the Defendant.

The following cases were cited in argument:—

> *Richards v. Rose*, (9 Ex. 218)
>
> *Rigby v. Bennett*, (L. R. 21 Ch. D. 559)
>
> *Allen v. Taylor*, (L. R. 16 Ch. D. 355)
>
> *Siddons v. Short*, (L. R. 2. C. P. D. 572)
>
> *Swansborough v. Coventry*, (9 Bing. 305)
>
> *Compton v. Richards*, (1 Price 27)
>
> *Corporation of Birmingham v. Allen*, (L. R. 6 Ch. D. 284)
>
> *Dodd v. Holme*, (1 Ad & El. 493)
>
> *Pinnington v. Galland*, (9. Ex. 1.)

BONSER, C. J.

This is an action brought by the owner of two houses, Nos. 104 and 105 Cheang Cheok Street, against the owner of the adjoining lots for damage done to these houses caused by an excavation which it was alleged was improperly made by the Defendant. The facts appear to be that the land on which the Plaintiff's houses were built and the Defendant's land originally belonged to the same owner, and that in the year 1877, the owner subdivided the estate into allotments for building purposes. On the 18th January, 1878, the Defendant's land was conveyed to a person named Emamsah, his predecessor in title, the owner retaining in his possession the lots on which the Plaintiff's houses are now built. It does not appear in the evidence nor in the admissions, what was the nature of the conveyance. It was merely spoken of as a conveyance, and therefore I draw the inference —on the evidence I am not entitled to do more—that it was an ordinary conveyance in fee, without any restrictive covenants or stipulations. It was alleged and admitted that at the time of the conveyance to Emamsah, Emamsah knew that the adjoining land, the lots on which the Plaintiff's houses were built, was intended to be used and was laid out for building purposes. Some months subsequent to the 1st May, 1878, the lots on which the houses Nos. 104 and 105 now

BONSER, C. J.

1893.

TAN MEE NEO
v.
TAN TIG

stand were conveyed by his predecessor in title to the Plaintiff, and
with regard to that I again draw the inference that it was a mere
conveyance in fee, without restrictive covenants and without any
provisions as to building. Some time subsequent to the 1st May,
1878, these houses were built, but the Defendant's predecessor in
title allowed his land to lie idle and nothing was built upon it.
But in June, 1893, the Defendant was minded to build on his piece
of land, and whether he employed a contractor or not—that was
immaterial—he proceeded to dig a trench on the edge of his land,
flush with the wall and foundations of the Plaintiff's house, No. 105,
which had been built on the extreme edge of his lot. That trench
was sunk to a depth of two feet, the extreme depth to which he intended
to go, as it appeared that he had commenced laying his foundations
in part of the trench. But shallow as that trench was it went a little
deeper than the foundations of the Plaintiff's house. The trench
apparently was dug on the 28th June, and on the night of the 28th
a very heavy rain shower came down, the trench being filled with
water and the sides of the trench in part collapsing so that the
Plaintiff's house came down. The Plaintiff alleged that this was
a direct consequence of the trench being dug, and it was suggested
by Mr. Joaquim, though I do not think the suggestion was supported
by, but was quite inconsistent with the facts, that this was a mere
coincidence; it seems quite incredible to me that if the trench had not
been dug at all the house would have fallen when it did. The foundations of the Plaintiff's house were very shallow. Mr. Lermit, I think,
said about a foot deep, and Mr. Cook said certainly not more than
eighteen inches; whilst it also appeared that in some places the
foundations of No. 105 had not been carried down to solid ground
but were raised on made earth. The foundations were, therefore,
not only shallow but not such as one would have expected; and Mr.
Lermit admitted in evidence that though the foundations were
sufficiently strong for that class of house, he would not have passed
these foundations if he had been superintending them at the time
they were laid. I consider that it was established, therefore, that the
foundations were not proper foundations. Then with regard to the
wall, all the witnesses, Plaintiff's and Defendant's professional witnesses, were agreed that the mortar was not good, and it was proved to
my satisfaction that the house was in a ruinous state. But as I re-

BONSER, C. J. marked in the course of the argument, if the Plaintiff's house had a
1893.
TAN MEE NEO
v.
TAN TUE. right to the support of the Defendant's land, the Defendant had no
right to accelerate its fall. There was also a claim for trespass, but there
was no evidence to support that, and I find that there was no trespass
committed on the Plaintiff's land. The law as to the right of support
was laid down in the case of *Dalton v. Angus*, (L. R. 6. App. C. 791,)
where it was said that the support necessary for land, without reference to buildings, was a natural right, but that when built upon,
a different state of things arose. Support to that which is artificially
imposed upon land is not a natural right, but must in each particular
case be acquired by grant, or by some means equivalent in law to
grant, in order to make it a burden upon the neighbour's land, which
would (naturally) be free from it.   In this case there was no question
of prescription, and the question arose whether the Plaintiff had
acquired for his house a right to support by grant or by some means
equivalent in law to grant.   That he had not acquired an express
grant was clear. With regard to adjoining tenements belonging to
different owners the law was quite clear.   It was stated by Lord Penzance in the same case in these words. " It is the law, I believe I may
say without question, that at any time within twenty years after the
house is built the owner of the adjacent soil may with perfect legality
dig that soil away, and allow his neighbour's house, if supported by
it, to fall in ruins to the ground. This being so, and these being his
legal rights (the rights incident to his ownership), it seems to me that
these rights must remain to him, or those who come after him, for all
time, unless he, or they, have done something by which these rights
have been divested, restricted or impaired."   But where the land had
been held by the same owners different considerations seemed to arise.
Lord Selborne said, " If at the time of the severance of the land from
that of the adjoining proprietor it was not in its original state, but
had buildings standing upon it up to the dividing line, or if it were
conveyed expressly with a view to the erection of such buildings, or to
any other use of it which might render increased support necessary,
then there would be an implied grant of such support as the actual
state or the contemplated use of the land would require, and the
artificial would be inseparable from, and (as between the parties to
the contract) would be a mere enlargement of the natural."   So that
if a person owning a piece of land built a house upon it, and then

conveyed that house, retaining an adjoining piece of land unbuilt upon, there would, although nothing was said about the right of support or lights, be an implied grant of support or lights. As regards lights, that is clearly laid down in *Allen v. Taylor*, (L. R. 16 Ch. D. 355.) But if the owner of a house and adjoining land sells the adjoining land and retains the house, can the purchaser excavate the land, so as to let the house down ? There seems to be no direct authority upon the point, but in my opinion he could not. The owner of the house may rest upon the principle that the right of support is necessary for the existence of the house and therefore there is an implied obligation not to deprive the house of that which is necessary for its existence and I think that *Pinnington v. Galland*, (9 Ex. 1.) is in point. But it was sought in the present case to carry that principle even further, and to say that the mere fact that land was sold for building purposes deprived the purchaser of dealing with it in the best way he could. I do not think there is any case which justified that conclusion. A man might have the present intention of building, and he might change his mind, nor was it necessary that he should build upon that land. The case where a house was already built was different, because there the thing existed, but in the case of land there was no binding necessity upon a man to use it in a particular way. Therefore, I do not think that the case of land unbuilt upon and reserved by the owner for building purposes, even if the purchaser knew that the owner intended to use it as building land, rests on the same principle as the case in which a house had already been built. With regard to the question of land being intended for building purposes I doubt whether under the circumstances this question could be taken into consideration. By the judgment of the Court in the case of *Wheeldon v. Burroughes* (L. R. 12 Ch. D. 31) I think it could not, and that I am not entitled to look back upon any arrangement between the parties. What might have been the result if all these pieces of land had been conveyed at the same time as part and parcel of one transaction is not for me to inquire, but the only fact before them that could lead them to the conclusion that the land was intended for building purposes is that it was laid out in allotments. The evidence was to the effect that there were no stipulations in the conveyance as to building rights, and being precluded from going into con-

BONSER, C. J.

1893.

TAN MEE NEO
v.
TAN TUG.

BONSER, C. J.   siderations as to the intended use of the property, there was no evid-
   1896.   ence that the Plaintiff's and the Defendant's predecessors in title
TAN MEE NEO   were brought together in any way, or that there was any privity
   v.   between them of any kind.   The only statement was that the property
TAN TOO.   was conveyed first to the Defendant, and that he knew when he took
his conveyance that the adjoining lots were intended to be built upon
and were alloted for building purposes.   Therefore, it seems to me that
the Plaintiff had no implied grant, he certainly had no express grant for
such support as the actual state or contemplated use of the land would
require.   Nor had he since acquired a right to burden the Defendant's
land with his building.   But even supposing he had, I think there is
still another difficulty in the Plaintiff's way.   It has been argued that
the parties, the owners of these adjacent lots, must have given each
other mutual implied rights of support, and that each person was
entitled only to use his land in a reasonable way.   The question
therefore arose whether the parties had used their land in a reasonable
way, and it seems to me that the Plaintiff has not used his land in a
reasonable way by building a house in the way he had upon the
extreme verge of his land.   If he did build on the extreme verge of
his land—as he had a perfect right to do—he ought to have taken
every care that his foundations were proper foundations, and the
evidence went to show that the foundations were not proper foundations.   Then, again, it was said the Defendant behaved in an unreasonable way.   There was not much evidence on that point, but it
does not seem to me that to dig a trench two feet deep was a very unreasonable way to use land.

[The Chief Justice then went on to consider the evidence offered
as to the practice or the necessity of shoring up the building or the
sides of the trench, coming to the conclusion that it was not an invariable custom with Chinese contractors to do so, and that if the house
had been properly built, or if the foundations had been properly laid,
the cutting of the trench would have had no effect upon the house].
Under the circumstances, therefore, I give judgment for the Defendant.

Solicitors for the Plaintiff.—*Donaldson & Burkinshaw.*

Solicitors for the Defendant.—*Joaquim Brothers.*

TAN CHENG.

v.

MURRAY.

[SINGAPORE.]

Contract—Warranty—Caveat Emptor.

By the instructions of the Defendant, who acted as owner of it, certain coffee saved from a godown which had been destroyed by fire was sold by auction by P. & Co. The day before the auction a circular in the Chinese language was circulated in which it was stated "These goods are from K's godown after the fire, have been slightly damaged by the water, but still nothing to prevent them being made use of." The Plaintiff received a copy of the notice and attended the auction, and after examining the coffee became the purchaser of a portion of it. After the sale but before the balance of the purchase money had been paid, the Defendant discovered that the coffee was impregnated with arsenic and unfit for consumption. P & Co. received the balance of the purchase money and paid it to the Defendant. In an action by the Plaintiff to recover his purchase money or damages for breach of warranty.

Held that the maxim *Caveat emptor* applied, and that the Plaintiff could not recover.

THE facts and arguments sufficiently appear from the judgment. *Napier* appeared for the Plaintiff and cited the following cases:—

> *Ward v. Hobbs*, (L. R. 4 App: C. 13).
>
> *Shelton v. Livius*, (2 Crompton and Jervis 411).
>
> *Shepherd v. Kain*, (5 B. & Ald. 240).
>
> *Peirce v. Corf*, (L. R. 9 Q. B. 210).
>
> *Brady v. Todd*, (9 C. B. N. S. 592).
>
> *Josling v. Kingsford*, (13 C. B. N. S. 447).
>
> *Hopkins v. Tanqueray*, (15 C. B. 130).

Nanson for the Defendant cited:—

> *Salmon v. Ward*, (2 Car & P. 211).
>
> *Chandelor v. Lopus*, (1 Smith's L. C. [9th Ed.] 186).
>
> *Stuckley v. Bailey*, (1 H. & C. 405).
>
> *Carnac v. Warriner*, (1 C. B. 356).
>
> *Pickering v. Dowson* (4 Taunt 786).

LOGAN. J.

1881.
Nov. 27 & 28
and
Dec. 4.

LOGAN, J.

This action arises out of a sale by auction on the 7th of July last, of certain bags of coffee, pepper, and cloves which had been saved from a fire that had occurred in the godown of Messrs. McKerrow & Co. on the 1st of that month. The day before that sale the auctioneer. who had been instructed by the Defendant (who was acting for the Insurance Companies affected by the fire) to take charge of the salvage and to realise, issued notices of the intended sale in the Chinese language. The translation of that notice is as follows :—

" Auction sale of sundry goods remaining after the fire. It is fixed that on the 7th day of the present English month..... ....to sell by auction 500 bags of coffee, 100 bags of black pepper and 19 bags cloves. These goods are from Messrs. McKerrow's godown after the fire, have been slightly damaged by water, but still nothing to prevent them being made use of. All persons who wish to buy will please call at the auction at the appointed time. This is for the information of all."

The Plaintiff and others who had received the notice attended the auction. The goods were exhibited in the auction room and examined by the persons present. Plaintiff admitted having sampled the coffee and described it as wet, dirty, discoloured and damaged by water. some of it charred by fire, and a good deal of it mixed with dirt and cinders but the inside of the berries appeared to be good, and in his opinion the coffee, when cleaned and dried, would have been saleable. Of that coffee Plaintiff bought 261 bags at prices ranging from $3.25 to $10.25 a pikul. It was also proved that at the sale the goods were described as salvage, and that no statement was made as to quality, nor any reference to the notice was given, and that no conditions or particulars of sale were posted up in the auction room or entered in the auctioneer's ledger.

After the sale Plaintiff removed his goods on payment of a portion of the purchase money, and on the following Monday he paid the remainder of the purchase money in accordance with his undertaking. It appears that on the day following the sale it was discovered by the Defendant that at the time of the fire a large quantity of arsenic in tins had been stored in a part of the godown and that some of the tins had burst through the heat. There was danger therefore that the articles which had been sold on the previous day had been contaminated by the arsenic. That information was not, however, communicated to the purchasers until the balance of the purchase money had been paid, but when that had been done the Defendant caused samples to be taken of the goods that had been sold, and had them tested, the result showing that all the coffee was more or less poisoned by arsenic. The police thereupon took possession of the coffee, with a view to preventing its sale for consumption and the coffee was subsequently destroyed. The Plaintiff, therefore, through his solicitors applied to the Defendants for a refund of the price paid for the coffee, on the ground that it was not capable of being used as described in the notice, but the Defendants repudiated any liability.

This action was then commenced to recover the sum of $1,203.11 for breach of the warranty contained in the notice.

At the hearing it was argued by Mr. Napier, who appeared for the Plaintiff, that as warranties were not ordinarily given on sales of salvage goods, it must be concluded that the statement in the notice that the articles were capable of being made use of was intended as a warranty; that such a conclusion was not unreasonable; that the Defendant knew or had the means of knowing what goods had been stored in the godown at the time of the fire and was therefore in a position to authorise the auctioneer to warrant the goods to be free from deleterious matters; that the notice having been issued with the view of inducing people to purchase, the Plaintiff was justified in assuming that the words were intended to guarantee against latent defects; and that the contract between the parties was the offer contained in the notice and the acceptance of the auctioneer by the bid and not what was written in the auctioneer's ledger, which had been shown in some respects not to have satisfied the requirements of the Statute of Frauds.

On the other hand, Mr. Nanson, for the Defendant, contended that the notice was nothing more than a commendation of the goods to be sold and an invitation to persons to attend a sale of salvage goods, and that the expression relied on was not a warranty, but what had been termed an antecedent representation made without fraud and formed no part of the contract which was afterwards concluded.

As it was not suggested that the Defendant or the auctioneer had, either at the time the notice was issued or when the sale took place, any knowledge or suspicion that arsenic had been stored in the godown, the sole question material to this case is whether the statement in the notice as to the quality of the goods was intended as a positive warranty of quality and to form part of the contract that might be made at the auction on the following day, and was by the plaintiff so understood, or whether the statement was a mere representation or description of the goods to be sold.

Having regard to the nature of the sale and the circumstances of the case, I do not consider I should be justified in coming to the conclusion that the words relied upon in the notice were intended as a warranty. They appear to be nothing more than a statement of the auctioneer's own opinion and belief of the articles so far as they appeared to him to be and what he believed them to be, but concerning which an intending purchaser was to exercise his own judgment. In my opinion the notice means nothing more than an announcement of a sale of salvage goods, with a commendation of them. That that was how the notice was understood by the Plaintiff is, I think, shown by what took place at the sale and by the action of the Plaintiff in regard to the goods. It is true that the defect in the coffee was latent and not discoverable on examination, but as it was not shown that the statement in the notice had not been made *bona fide*, there does not appear to me to be anything in the circumstances of the case to take it out of the rule *caveat emptor*. This was the opinion I had formed of the case at the trial, but in view of the hardship of such a result on the Plaintiff I took time to consider, but I am sorry I am unable to arrive at a conclusion more in accord with the merits of the case.

I decide, therefore, that the Plaintiff has failed to prove a warranty, and there must be judgment for the Defendant. But in view of the unconscionable conduct of the Insurance Offices represented by the Defendant, I give no costs.

Solicitors for the Plaintiff—*Drew and Napier.*

Solicitors for the Defendant—*Rodyk and Davidson.*

THE QUEEN ON THE PROSECUTION OF
C. Q. G. CRAUFURD

v.

LEE AH BOON.

[SINGAPORE.]

Fishing Stakes outside limits of Port—Harbours Ordinance—Ordinance VIII of 1872 sec. 37—Port Rules of 12th December 1877.

Section 37 of Ordinance VIII of 1872 (The Harbours Ordinance of 1872) extends to fishing stakes erected outside the limits of the Port of Singapore as defined by the Port Rules of the 12th of December 1877.

THIS was a case stated on Appeal under section 18 of Ordinance XII of 1879 by C. W. S. Kynnersley, Esq., Magistrate of Police, Singapore, and directed by Bonser, C. J. to be argued before the full Court of Appeal.

C. A.

COX, C. J.
GATTY AND
LAW. JJ.

1894.
Feb 2d.

Bromhead-Matthews appeared for Lee Ah Boon, the Appellant.

The *Attorney-General* appeared for the Respondent.

The Appellant was convicted on the 4th October, 1893, for that he on or about the 15th August, 1893, at Singapore did erect a fishing stake within 200 fathoms of a fishing stake already erected at Pulau Propoh in breach of Rule I of the " Fishing Stakes Rules " made by the Governor in Council under section 37 of Ordinance VIII of 1872.

The Appellant was fined $10 and costs. The ground of Appeal were that :—

1. The verdict was against the weight of evidence.

2. The fishing stakes Rules sanctioned by the Governor in Council under section 37 of the Harbours Ordinance 1872 did not apply to fishing stakes beyond the Harbour Limits.

3. The Magistrate had no jurisdiction to try the case.

4. The matter complained of was not punishable under any law in force in the Colony.

Bromhead-Matthews. This case was directed by Bonser, C. J. to be argued before the Court of Appeal under section 38 of the Appeals Ordinance 1879.

[*GATTY, J.* No order to that effect appears on the Record.]

Bromhead-Matthews. The learned Chief Justice made an order to that effect and a note appears on the papers.

[*GATTY, J.* A proper order should have been drawn up as in its absence there is nothing to guide the Court as to whether the whole case is to be argued or a particular point of Law only.]

Bromhead-Matthews. It is admitted that the fishing stakes in question are seven or eight miles beyond Harbour Limits, therefore Ordinance VIII of 1872 does not apply and the conviction must be quashed.

Ordinance VIII of 1872 is intituled an " Ordinance for the Regulation of Ports and Harbours " and the preamble shows that the Ordinance was passed to make better provisions for the regulations of

C. A.
COX, C. J.
GATTY, AND
LAW, JJ.
1891.
THE QUEEN ON
THE
PROSECUTION
OF
C. Q. G. CRAU-
FURD
v.
LEE AH BOON.

Ports and Harbours of the Colony and the navigable rivers and channels leading thereto. Section 4 shows that only such of the Ports and Harbours, &c as are declared by the Governor in Council to be subject to the Ordinance come within its purview, and this section as well as sections 5, 6, 7 & 8 shows that the Governor's powers of declaration are limited to the Ports, Harbours &c.

Nearly every section of the Ordinance refers to the Ports, Harbours &c, *subject to this Ordinance*, i. e. subject as provided by section 4 and the following sections. All the Rules made by the Governor in Council under this Ordinance appear in the Gazette as " Port Rules" and the rule relating to fishing stakes appears under this head of " Port Rules."

The words " at the several Settlements " appearing in section 37 of the Ordinance are inconsistent with the rest of the Ordinance and the words " Ports, Harbours & navigable rivers and channels leading thereto " must be read into the sections before those words, and this was the intention of the Legislature as seen from the title and preamble (*see Maxwell* on Interpretation of Statutes pp. 34 & 35) *Claydon v. Green* (L. R. 3 C. P. 511), *Barrow v. Madkin* (24 Beav. 327), *Beard v. Rowan* (9 Peters 317).

If the Ordinance refers to the whole Settlement there is no necessity for section 4, as all Ports & Harbours &c. within the Settlement would be included.

The object of the Ordinance was to facilitate navigation in Ports and Harbours &c., these fishing stakes are several miles out of the ordinary course of navigation and thus regulation is not necessary.

By section 37 obstructions or unlawful erections are to be pulled down by the Conservator of the Port and by section 8 his powers are limited to the Ports, Harbours and navigable rivers and channels leading thereto subject to the Ordinance.

Secondly, if I am wrong on the first point, section 37 enacts that the Governor in Council may make Rules and Orders for the erection &c., of fishing stakes at the several Settlements, prescribing the *places where the same may be erected.* Until the Governor in Council has prescribed such places there can be no offence in erecting them anywhere within the Settlement. The Governor in Council has so far not prescribed any places where they may be erected and unless the conviction is quashed every fishing stake erected in this Settlement has been illegally erected.

Thirdly, on the facts the Appellant committed no offence because when he erected the fishing stake in question he had a license from the Master Attendant so to do. In fact both parties had licenses.

The Attorney-General. This Ordinance is not limited to Ports and Harbours &c., though part of it may be. Sections 27, 41, & 43 refer to matters outside the Harbour Limits, and sections 27 and 43 to matters outside the Settlement and section 37 applies to fishing stakes within the Settlement even though outside Harbour Limits. There is no ambiguity about the word "Settlement" in section 37 and it must be given its ordinary meaning.

As to the Appellant's first point, Ordinance V. of 1891 which is an amending Ordinance, though in section 11 it alters the word "Settlement" into "Port," has left section 37 as it was.

As to the Appellant's third point, the license was granted under a misapprehension and even if he had a license he should still have complied with the Rules subject to which it was granted.

As to the second point, until the Governor prescribed places where fishing stakes may be erected they can be erected anywhere in the Settlement subject to the Rules made by the Governor in Council. The conviction should be upheld.

Bromhead-Matthews in reply. The Rules made by the Governor in Council are of no effect until the places to which they are to apply are prescribed.

COX, C. J.

The conviction cannot be quashed, but the fine of $ 10 will be reduced to $ 1 and no costs will be given of this Appeal but the Respondent will be entitled to his costs in the Court below.

Section 37 applies to fishing stakes within the several Settlements and is not restricted to the Ports and Harbours &c.

There is no ambiguity about the words "several Settlements" and that being so there is no necessity to look at the title and preamble to the Ordinance. In section 43 "Colonial Waters" are mentioned which clearly shows that the purview of the Ordinance is not limited to Ports and Harbours &c.

GATTY, J.

Fishing stakes erected within the several Settlements are within section 37 and the conviction must be affirmed subject to the reduc-

C. A.

COX, C. J.
GATTY AND
LAW, JJ.

1894.

THE QUEEN ON
THE
PROSECUTION
OF
C. Q. G. CRAU-
FURD
v.
LEE AH BOON.

C. A.
COX, C. J.
GATTY, AND
LAW, JJ.
——
1894
——
THE QUEEN ON
THE
PROSECUTION
OF
C. Q. G. CRAU-
FURD
v.
LEE AH BOON.

tion mentioned by the Chief Justice.

LAW, J.

I concur.

Conviction affirmed, but fine reduced to $ 1.   No costs of Appeal.

Solicitor for the Appellant.—W. C. Niblett.

CHOP BAN GUAN LEONG

v.

QUAIK KONG.

[SINGAPORE.]

Costs—Pauper—Civil Procedure Ordinance sec. 461—Advocates and Solicitors' Costs (Ordinance XVII of 1886)—Law and principles of taxation—Leave to appeal in formâ pauperis.

Section 461 of the Civil Procedure Ordinance (V of 1878) gives the Advocate and Solicitor assigned to a pauper a statutory right to his fees when costs have been awarded to be paid by the unsuccessful party, and is not repealed expressly or impliedly by section 2, sub-sec. (3) of Ordinance XVII of 1886 which deals with the "taxation of costs."

A party once admitted to sue or defend in formâ pauperis can appeal without leave to appeal as a pauper.

Drennnan v. Andrew (L. R. 1 Ch. App. 300) followed.

C. A.
——
GATTY
AND
LAW, JJ.
——
1894.
March 5.

THIS was an Appeal from the decision of Cox, C. J. reported supra p. 24.

On the Appeal being called on

Buckley for the Respondent, the Plaintiff in the action, raised the preliminary objection that by sec. 21 of the Appeals Ordinance of 1893 a pauper must obtain leave to appeal.   No such leave had been given. It was a condition precedent and unfulfilled.

R. W. Braddell for the Appellant.   When once admitted to sue or defend in formâ pauperis leave is not necessary to carry the pauper through all subsequent stages.   The law here is identical with the practice formerly existing in the English Courts.   *Drennan v. Andrew* (L. R. 1 Ch. App. 300).   If this case does not apply, the Court has full powers of amendment and can make the order now without prejudicing the Respondent.

[The Court (GATTY and LAW JJ.) ruled that leave to appeal in formâ pauperis was not necessary and that the original order to defend in formâ pauperis carried the pauper through all stages.]

C. A.

GATTY
AND
LAW, JJ.

1894.

CHOP BAN GUAN
LEONG
v.
QUAIK KONG.

Braddell in support of the Appeal. Section 461 of the Civil Procedure Ordinance entitles the Advocate and Solicitor assigned to a pauper to recover his fees in the event of the Court awarding costs against the unsuccessful party. It first prohibits him from receiving any fee i.e. recompense for his services, and if the section stopped here the English cases would apply, but it goes on in the same sentence and expressly entitles him to those very fees if his client succeeds, and costs are awarded to be paid by his opponent. The same with regard to the Court fees. At the time this section was passed the practice in the Courts of Chancery was to allow Counsel fees and remuneration to Solicitors on the ground that Counsel and Solicitor gave their services to the pauper only and not to his opponent. *Rattray v. George* (16 Ves. 232), *Wallop v. Warburton* (2. Cox. Ch. Cases 409). The Respondent does not object to pay these and the Registrar has demanded them. The learned Judge in the Court below admits the difficulty of reconciling this section with the English cases but decides the case upon sec. 2 sub-sec. (3) of Ordinance XVII of 1886. It is unfortunate that this point was not argued or referred to in the Court below, but this Ordinance does not apply to the fees of the Advocate and Solicitor to be allowed under sec. 461. It does not repeal that section expressly nor does it do so impliedly. Section 461 is a special law governing a particular right to which the Legislature has given special attention. The Ordinance of 1886 is a general act and does not repeal a special act (*Maxwell* on Statutes).

Ordinance XVII of 1886 only applies to costs as defined in sub-sec. 7 which are all moneys, by whatever name called, that a client pays or is liable to pay to an Advocate and Solicitor. Here the pauper is not liable to pay his Advocate and Solicitor in any event. The costs and fees are to be recovered only from the opponent in the same way that the Court fees are to be recovered. Sec. 24 of the Courts Ordinance (III of 1878) settles any doubt there may be as to whence the Court fees are to be recovered. Sec. 2 sub sec. (3) of Ordinance XVII of 1886 cannot be read with sec. 461 without repealing it; and it is clearly not repealed because its provisions are embodied in the Appeals Ordinance of 1893 drawn by the same learned draughtsman. It cannot be

C. A.
———
GATTY
AND
LAW, JJ.
———
1894.
———
CHOP BAN GUAN
LEONG
v.
QUAIK KONG.

argued that the practice and procedure as to the costs of pauper appeals in England apply to this Court because of the joint operation of sections 21 and 37 of the Appeals Ordinance of 1893 ; so that if the judgment of the Court below stands, we shall be in the absurd position of having the Advocate and Solicitor entitled to his fees in the Court of Appeal but not in the Supreme Court.

Buckley. Section 461 gives no absolute right, it only says that the Solicitor shall be entitled to what shall be allowed on taxation. If he is allowed nothing on taxation, he can get nothing. It is a question of how the bill is to be taxed. Sec. 52 of the Courts Ordinance (III of 1878) said that costs were to be taxed in the same manner as in England ; this might refer to the method of procedure only, as to giving notice and so forth. But it had been repealed and a much wider section enacted in its place by sec. 2 of Ordinance XVII of 1886 on which the Chief Justice relied in his judgment. That section provided for party and party as well as for Solicitor and client's costs, and therefore included all costs in contested cases. And it said that the taxation of costs was to be governed by and conducted upon the law and principles as in England. The Registrar, when the bill of costs in this matter was brought before him for taxation, had therefore to tax it on that law and principles and on no other. The words "law and principles" were very wide indeed, they meant a great deal more than the words "in the same manner as in England" in the section that had been repealed. There was no doubt whatever what the law in England was as to pauper costs. As long back as 400 years ago, in 1494, in the reign of Henry VII, it had been enacted that no person assigned to a pauper could receive any fees, and eminent judges had expressed the opinion that to allow any fees to be taken was bad morally as well as legally. The matter was before the House of Lords, in the case referred to by the Chief Justice, in 1892, and it was held that only costs out of pocket and a reasonable sum for clerks' expenses should be allowed, on the ground that although the Solicitor gave his services for nothing, it was not right that he should be out of pocket as well. The principle on which the law rested might be seen from the judgment of Lord Campbell C. J. in *Dooly v. The Great Northern Railway Co.,* (4 E. & B. 341) in which he said :—

"It seems to me impossible to say that our decision either conflicts

C. A.

GAT₁Y
AND
LAW, JJ

1894.

CHOP BAN GUAN
LEONG
r.
QUAIK KONG

with the statutes, or is injurious to any one.   The Statute of Glouces-
ter (a) gave the Plaintiff recovering damages the costs of his writ,
and that has always been construed as including all the costs expended
in consequence of the defence by the Defendant.   Then has not this
Plaintiff been allowed all that she has paid or become liable to pay in
consequence of the defence ?   How can it be said that she was liable
either at law or in honour to pay those rewards which stat. 11. H.
7. c. 12 expressly (and I think most judiciously) says shall not be paid.
A practice to the contrary had grown up; I agree with my
brother Erle that it was contrary to law.   I regret that it prevailed
so long; and I am confident no evil need be apprehended from its
discontinuance.   No pauper having a real just cause of action will
ever fail to find respectable members of both branches of the profession ready to assist gratuitously in the furtherance of justice.   If it
should be necessary, the Court has power to assign both.   But all
members of this honourable profession are not honourable; and great
evil did arise from the manner in which some did abuse the power
to conduct suits in formâ pauperis.   When first I became Chief
Justice, I found the evil prevailing to a frightful extent.   It is no
exaggeration to say that at every sittings in Middlesex there were
expensive actions for malicious prosecutions brought in formâ pauperis by felons acquitted only on some technical ground.   To meet
this evil the Judges made the rule referred to, which seems to me only
to restore the practice to that which by law it ought always to have
been."

   And in *Carson v. Pickersgill.* (L. R. 14 Q. B. D. 859) the Master
of the Rolls in his judgment referring to the above passage spoke of
the practice as being contrary to the ethical rules of right and wrong.
The petition to the House of Lords in the case of *Johnson v. Lindsay,*
(L. R. [1892] A. C. 110) is to be found at length on page 88 of the
Law Times for 1892, and puts very fully the objections to allowing
such costs.   Under Order 16 rule 31 of the English rules, costs in
such cases are " to be taxed as in other cases", but these words were
held to be restricted by the rule of law which for 400 years had for-
bidden such costs to be paid.

   Braddell in reply.   *Carson v. Pickesgill* (L. R. 14 Q. B. D. 859)
is an authority against the pauper recovering and does not touch the
Advocate and Solicitor, but the dicta in that case are in favour of this

C. A
GATTY
AND
LAW, JJ.
1894.

CHOP BAN GUAN
LEONG
v.
QUAIK KONG.

Appeal. (*see* Grove, J. on p. 863 " what a strange construction &c."
and " The only other question" to the end.)

GATTY. J.

This is an Appeal from a decision of the Chief Justice made by
him upon the hearing of an Appeal from a decision of the Registrar
in Chambers on taxation of costs in a debtor suit, and the substantive
question raised before the Court of Appeal was whether or not an Advocate or Solicitor of that Court who had been assigned by the Court
to prosecute or defend a case for a pauper was entitled to receive any
fee in the event of the Court allowing costs against the unsuccessful
party and in favour of the pauper. A great deal depended upon the
construction to be put upon sec. 461 of the Civil Procedure Ordinance.
and in fact I think that the whole case depends upon the construction
which the Court puts upon that section. That section indicates, in
the first place, that no fee is to be taken by any Advocate or Solicitor
assigned by the Court, and distinctly prohibits the Solicitor or Advocate from taking any fee or receiving any reward for his services
when acting for a debtor. The next words in the section prohibit the
Court officials from demanding any Court fees from any person applying or admitted to sue or defend as a pauper. Then we
come to the exception " but if he succeed, and costs should be awarded
to be paid by his opponent then the Advocate and Solicitor
so assigned shall be entitled to, and shall receive, all such fees as the
Registrar of the Court shall allow him on taxation, and such Court
fees as would in other cases be chargeable shall be charged and
recovered." From the wording of this latter part of the section it
seems to me clear that the Legislature when they enacted section 461
of the Ordinance intended that in certain cases the Advocate or
Solicitor should receive a fee or reward for his services, and that the
Court fees which would otherwise be chargeable should be recovered.
This is not a case in which the Legislature has merely said, if he
succeed, any one suing or defending on behalf of a pauper shall be
entitled to costs as in other cases. as on the wording of the section
I hold that these words " shall be entitled to " give a statutory right
to the Advocate or Solicitor who is employed in a pauper suit to receive some reward or fee, and expressly imposes upon the Court officials
the duty of collecting the same Court fees as would in other cases
be chargeable, if the case were not a pauper suit. But this it was

said had been repealed by the enactment of Ordinance XVII of 1886 sec. 2, sub-sec. (3), which provides that the taxation of the costs of Advocates and Solicitors shall be governed by and conducted upon the law and principles by and upon which the taxation of costs is for the time being governed and conducted in the Supreme Court of Judicature in England. On looking at the definition of costs I find that such a bill as was mentioned in sec. 461 is not included in that definition, it includes certain fees which were payable by a person who employed a Solicitor or Advocate, but does not include this case. I hold that sec. 461 conveys a statutory right to a fee, but I do not rest my judgment entirely on that in holding that the express words of sec. 461 have not been repealed by the Ordinance of 1886. It seems to me that the law or rules governing taxation in England did not and never could have been intended to take away an existing right to any fee or costs here. Ordinance XVII of 1886 was only for the definition and limitation of rights which already existed under some other authority. It would be far too much to give such a meaning to the words "law and principles by and upon which taxation" was governed as to hold that a law enacted in England should take away an express right given, as I hold, under sec. 461 of the Civil Procedure Ordinance; and that I find is quite in consonance with the expressions used by Grove, J. in *Carson v. Pickersgill* (L.R. 14 Q.B.D. 859). I am therefore of opinion that the words in section 461 which say that the Registrar is to allow the Advocate or Solicitor such a fee does not mean such fees as the Registrar should allow him on taxation of costs, but it meant such a reasonable fee as the Registrar should allow on taxing that fee, not on taxing costs. The taxation of this fee had nothing on earth to do with the taxation of the costs in the suit. The right to a fee was given by the Statute. It arose in the cases mentioned by the Statute, in cases where the Court had awarded costs. The right did not arise from the Judge's order, it arose from the Statute and there was a statutory duty imposed on the Registrar of taxing that fee. I find no difficulty in coming to this conclusion, and I do not find that the English law and the English cases really touch the point, because they had not such a provision as section 461, without which there could be no doubt that the Solicitor would not be entitled to these costs. But I hold there is something here which does not exist

C. A.

GATTY
AND
LAW, JJ.

1894.

CHOP BAN GUAN
LEONG
v.
QUAIK KONG.

C. A.
GATTY
AND
LAW, JJ.
1894.
CHOP BAN GUAN
LEONG
v.
QUAIK KONG.

in the British law, which does exist in the Colonial law, and it was.
further. a right which was not taken away by that section of the
Advocates and Solicitors Ordinance. which merely indicated that the
law and rules governing taxation of costs in England should be followed in this Colony. It is quite conceivable. though I do not know
of such a case, that some other fee may be chargeable under some law
of the Colony which would not be recoverable under the law in England. In my opinion the judgment of the Chief Justice ought to be
reversed. I hold that under the circumstances mentioned in the
Ordinance there is a statutory right given to the Advocate or Solicitor
to a fee, that the taxation of this fee had nothing to do with the
taxation by the Registrar of the costs of the suit, and that the
Registrar ought to be directed to allow a fee to Advocates and Solicitors in these cases.

LAW, J.

I concur. I think the intention of sec. 461 of the Civil Procedure
Ordinance was to give a right to a fee. I do not think this fee was
included in the fees mentioned in sec. 2, sub-sec. (3), of Ordinance
XVII of 1886, and therefore on this ground I do not think the right
has been taken away. For these reasons I think the judgment ought
to be reversed.

R. W. Braddell applied for costs of the appeal. but these were
disallowed.

Solicitors for the Plaintiff.—*Rodyk and Davidson.*

Solicitors for the Defendant.—*Braddell Brothers and Matthews.*

CHONG MOH & Co., *v. S. S. CAMELOT.*

AND

THE CAMELOT STEAMSHIP Co. LTD., *v. S. S. DIAMOND.*

[SINGAPORE.]

Admiralty—Interest on damages where both ships are to blame.

In an Admiralty action where both ships have been held to blame
in finally adjusting the accounts as between the parties, interest at the rate
of 8 per cent per annum must be calculated on the amounts of damage
sustained by each as from the date in which interest would have been payable in case the other ship had been held solely to blame.

LAW, J.
1894.
March 13 & 14,

THIS case which is reported in S. S. L. R. (1893) 119 is an action
for damage arising out of a collision. The damage sustained

by the S. S. *Camelot*, was found by the Registrar's certificate, as ultimately settled, to amount to the sum of $47,747.30 " with interest from the 15th day of August, 1892, (the date of the payment of the dock bill) at the rate of eight per cent per annum until paid." The damage sustained by the S. S. *Diamond*, as found by the Registrar's certificate amounted to $38,801.09 " with interest thereon from the 17th of August, 1892," (the date of the payment of the dock bill). The present application was for an order on the owners of the S. S. *Diamond*, to pay the balance due to the owners of the S. S. *Camelot*. and the question arose as to interest. The owners of the S. S. *Camelot* intended that the interest should be calculated on both amounts of damage from the respective days mentioned in the certificates to the day of payment, and that the owners of the S. S. *Camelot* should recover the difference between her damages including interest and one half the total damage including interest sustained by both ships.

LAW, J.
1894.
CHONG
MOH & CO.
v
S.S. "CAMELOT"
AND THE
CAMELOT
STEAMSHIP CO.,
LTD.,
r.
S.S. "DIAMOND."

Drew for the owners of the S. S. *Camelot*. Interest has been found as a part of the damages by the Registrar. Interest is always payable on damage arising from a collision. The *Hebe*. (2 W.. Rob. 146.)

Nanson on behalf of the owners of the S. S. *Diamond* contended that interest was only payable from the date of the order of the Court of Appeal (14th June, 1893.) The general rule as to damages does not extend to the case where both ships are to blame. He cited the remarks of Lord Selborne in *Stoomvaart Maatschappij Netherland v. P. & O. S. N. Co.* (L. R. 7. App. C. 795) on page 802.

Cur. Adv. Vult.

LAW, J.

In this matter it seems to me that it is hardly disputed that if one ship is held solely to blame, the damaged party is always entitled to interest on the amount of damage sustained from the date of payment for repairs and not from the date of the decree. When both ships are held to blame one would expect to find the rule the same, and I don't think any case has been cited on behalf of the S. S. *Diamond* sufficient to lead me to find that the rule is otherwise when both ships are to blame.

Solicitors for the S. S. *Camelot—Drew & Napier*
Solicitors for the S. S. *Diamond—Rodyk & Davidson*.

HUTTENBACH.

v.

WRIGHT & OTHERS.

[PENANG.]

Election—Legislative Council—Chamber of Commerce—Nomination—Franchise—Injunction—Jurisdiction—Costs.

The Penang Chamber of Commerce having been invited by the Governor of the Colony (in accordance with the Secretary of State's Despatch of 7th December 1887) to submit to him for approval the name of a gentleman to fill a vacancy in the Legislative Council, and the Chamber having under its own rules held two ballots for the purpose of electing its nominee, the first resulting in the election of B, and the second in the election of H, declared H, nominated ; but the Defendants (the Chairman and Committee of the Chamber) being advised that the second ballot was void, subsequently notified their intention of declaring B the nominee of the Chamber.   In an action by H against the Defendants claiming an injunction to restrain them from so doing.

Held (1) that H, (the Plaintiff) had no legal right which had been or could be injured so as to give the Court jurisdiction to interfere by injunction.   (2) that there were no legal duties attaching to the Chamber or its officers in respect to the mode in which they carried out the Governor's invitation or ascertained their nominee, (3) that the said invitation did not confer any legal right or franchise upon the Chamber nor constitute its members public officers nor impose upon them ministerial duties ; and (4) that the choice of a name by the Chamber to be submitted for approval was a step in the performance of an executive act and savoured of the exercise of political functions which it would be improper for the Court to interfere with.

The Court has jurisdiction to award costs even when it has no jurisdiction to give the relief claimed in the action.

GATTY, J.
1893.
Dec. 4, 5, 12
& 13.

THE nature and facts of this case sufficiently appear from the judgment.

Adams, for the Plaintiff.   The Plaintiff has a right which is being injured and the Court has therefore jurisdiction to issue an injunction.   The delegation contained in the Governor's letter to the Chamber of Commerce constitutes that body an electorate, and confers on them a privilege to be exercised as trustees for the public.   The trust so delegated cannot be carried out except on legal principles. The power of nomination when exercised creates a civil right in the person nominated.   This right also involves a question of property, as a Member of Council has a voice in the disposal of the revenue of the Colony.

GATTY, J.

1893,

HUTTENBACH.
".
WRIGHT &
OTHERS.

Kerr on Injunctions. 3rd Ed. p. 1.

Ordinance IV of 1878 sec. 2, sub-sec. 8.

North London Railway Coy. v. Great Northern Railway Coy. (L. R. 11 Q. B. D. 30.)

Beddow v. Beddow, (L. R. 9 Ch. D. 89.)

Aslatt v. Corporation of Southampton (L. R. 16 Ch. D. 143.)

The Plaintiff has a legal right to have the effect of his declaration as nominee of the Chamber carried out.

Ashby v. White. (2 Sm. L. C. 264.)

[*GATTY J.* In that case there was a franchise.]

The Chamber has a franchise, which is being improperly interfered with by the Committee in defiance of the wishes of the majority of the members. *Harben v. Phillips,* (L. R. 23 Ch. D. 14.)

Ross (*Clutton* and *Scott* with him) for the Defendants. The Court has no jurisdiction to grant this injunction, for sec. 2, subsec. 8 of Ordinance IV of 1878 confers no power on the Court to grant an injunction in cases where there is otherwise no legal remedy for the alleged wrong. *North London Railway Coy. v. Great Northern Railway Coy.* (supra.)

Britain v. Rossiter (L. R. 11 Q. B. D. 123.)

Aslatt v. Corporation of Southampton (supra) is distinguishable. In that case there was an office and a question of property as well as personal status involved. The later case of *Richardson v. Methley School Board* (69 L. T. N. S. 308) is also distinguishable on similar grounds. There was no legal duty imposed on the Chamber to nominate and therefore no power in this Court to compel them to do so.

The Queen v. Hertford College (L. R. 3 Q. B. D. 693.)

If the Defendants were wrong in their proceeding it was futile and productive of no injury, and the Court would not issue an injunction.

London and Blackwall Railway Coy. v. Cross (L. R. 31 Ch. D. 354.)

Farrar v. Cooper (L. R. 44 Ch. D. 323.)

Harper v. Paget (unreported) referred to in L. R. 44 Ch. D. at p. 328.

Even if nominated the Plaintiff might not be appointed by the Governor, he only obtains a chance of being so appointed. Such chance is not a right recognizable by law.

Chamberlain v. Boyd. (L. R. 11 Q. B. D. 407.)

When the official letters put in are closely examined it will be seen that they do not confer an electoral franchise on the Chamber and therefore *Ashby v. White* and *Harben v. Phillips* do not apply. The Chamber was merely the agent or delegate of the Governor, and as the Court would not interfere with His Excellency in performing an executive Act, it would not interfere with the Chamber or the Defendants, its Committee.

Adams in reply. The right conferred on the Chamber was not merely a franchise in its narrower sense, *i. e.* a right to nominate but was a distinctive grant by the Crown through the Governor to the Chamber. 29 & 30 Vic. c. 115 sec. 3. Letters Patent 17th June, 1885. The Secretary of States' Despatch of 7th December, 1887; and the Colonial Secretary's letter to the Chamber. The Chamber are *quasi* public officers as soon as they have accepted the Governor's invitation to nominate, and the Court can control their actions, which ar ministerial.

Shortt on Mandamus 252,260.

Reg v. Collins (L. R. 2. Q. B. D. 30.)

[*GATTY, J.* I would like to hear you, Mr. Ross, on the point raised by Mr. Adams as to the Chamber having a franchise by grant.]

Ross. The despatch of the Secretary of State is not under seal and therefore could not be a grant. The grant of a franchise, right or liberty can only be conferred by grant, that is, by a Deed under seal.

C. A. V.

GATTY, J.

In this case the plaintiff asks the Court to restrain by injunction the Chairman and Committee of the Penang Chamber of Commerce from holding the special meeting of the Chamber of Commerce which the Chairman has convened for the 29th November instant, for the purpose of declaring Dr. Brown to be the duly elected nominee of the said Chamber to the vacant seat in the Legislative Council of the Colony, and restraining generally the defendants and each of them and all other persons acting on their or either of their behalf from otherwise declaring Dr. Brown to be such duly elected nominee as aforesaid or otherwise interfering with the election of the plaintiff as such nominee as aforesaid. It was admitted, thouhg not proved in evidence, before the Court that the Penang Chamber of Commerce is a voluntary association of gentlemen not incorporated by any law or harter. The circumstances under which the Chamber proceeds to the nomination of a person for a seat in the Legislative Council appear to be as follows. In December, 1887, the then Secretary of State for the Colonies wrote a despatch to the Governor of this Colony in the following terms: "As regards the second nomination I prefer to "place it in the hands of the Penang Chamber of Commerce, and you "will accordingly, as occasion arises, invite the Chambers of Com- "merce of Singapore or of Penang to submit to you for approval the "name of a gentleman to fill a vacancy in the Council," and there- upon a letter was addressed by the Acting Colonial Secretary to the Chairman of the Chamber of Commerce in these words:—

COLONIAL SECRETARY'S OFFICE.
Singapore, 17th November, 1887.

The Chairman, Chamber of Commerce, Penang.

SIR,—I am directed by the Governor to inform you that it is in- tended, when the next vacancy among the Unofficial Members of the Legislative Council who more especially represent Penang occurs, to request the Chamber of Commerce, Penang, to nominate a member to fill such vacancy.

2. Further I am to state to you that in future Unofficial Mem- bers of the Legislative Council will hold their appointments for three years, but will be eligible for re-nomination.

I am, &c.,
A. M. SKINNER.
Acting Colonial Secretary, N. S

On the occasion in question in this action the Penang Chamber of Commerce had been invited accordingly to submit to the Governor the name of a gentleman to take the seat in the Legislative Council vacated by the death of a Mr. Comrie who had been previously nomi- nated by the Chamber and whose nomination had been in due course approved with the result that he was appointed to be a member of the Legislative Council under the letters patent of the Crown, re- gulating the constitution of the Legislature.

It was contended for the Plaintiff that the Chamber of Commerce having on a day previous to the writ in this action proceeded in response to the invitation from the executive to choose a name to be submitted to the Governor for approval, and the Chairman having on that occasion declared the Plaintiff to be the nominee of the Chamber, he, the plaintiff, had acquired a legal right which this Court had jurisdiction to protect by injunction from disturbance, and that ministerial duties attached to the Chairman and Committee of the Chamber the performance of which this Court had jurisdiction to insist upon by writ of mandamus or injunction.

It appears that the Chamber of Commerce had framed for itself a rule regulating the proceedings to be taken on such nominations in the following terms :—

1.—A Special General Meeting of the Chamber shall be called by Circular or by Advertisement in the Newspapers, stating that the object of the Meeting is to propose a nominee. At that Meeting it shall be competent for any Member to propose the name of any person or persons, which on being seconded shall be exhibited in a prominent place in the Exchange Room, or such other public room as may at the time be the usual meeting place of the Chamber, and may be otherwise publicly made known to members in such manner as the Committee may direct.

2.—At a second Special General Meeting to be held at an interval of not less than ten days from the first, a vote shall be taken, on the name or names proposed and on them alone. The vote shall be taken by a show of hands, or in the event of there being more than one person proposed, by a show of hands or by ballot, as the majority present at the Meeting may decide ; and the person receiving most votes shall be declared the nominee of the Chamber.

3.—In voting for a nominee for the Legislative Council, each Member or firm shall have but one vote, however many names may be proposed, except the Chairman, who shall have a casting vote as prescribed by Rule 7.

And on the day in question two ballots had been taken resulting differently, and as to the effect of which a difference of opinion arose resulting in the proposal by the Chairman and Committee of the Chamber to treat that which was taken last as a nullity and the first as a proper expression of the will of the Chamber in the matter of this nomination.

Under the above circumstances I am clearly of opinion that the plaintiff has not made out any case entitling him to claim the interference of this Court by injunction. The remedy by injunction is appropriate only in cases where there is a clear legal right to be pro-

tected. The Courts have seldom if ever granted this kind of relief
in any case where there was not injury either actual or prospective to
civil property. There is absolutely no question involving property in
this case, nor can I find any legal right existing in the plaintiff which
has been or can be injured so as to give the Court jurisdiction.

In my judgment there are no legal duties attaching either to the
Chamber of Commerce or its officers in respect of the exercise of the
permission or invitation to submit a name for approval given to them
under the instructions of the Secretary of State. The Chairman and
Committee in the Chamber cannot be regarded as public officers
whose acts can be interfered with or regulated by this Court. There
are no duties imposed upon them either by statute or by charter or by
any law. No authority has been cited to show that a Court of Law
has ever interfered by injunction or mandamus where a legal right in
the applicant or a legal obligation in the persons against whom the
writ is sought has not been shown to exist. I cannot regard the invitation to the Chamber of Commerce to submit a name as conferring
any legal right or franchise upon either the Chamber of Commerce as
a whole or any individual member of it. The prerogative of appointing members of the Legislative Council remains in the Crown, and no
law, charter, or document under the Great Seal has been shown in this
case to exist whereby any portion of that prerogative has been given
to any one else.

This is a case totally different from those in which the power or
duty of electing or nominating to an office has been given by statute,
law, or charter. There are no ministerial duties imposed upon the
Chamber or its officers or any member of it having their foundation
in law. The Chamber has been invited, not compelled, to submit a
name for approval. The method or process of choosing the name has
been left entirely to the Chamber. No regulations, having any legal
force, for ascertaining the will of the Chamber have been laid down
by the Executive. It is true that the Chamber has formed a rule for
its own guidance in the matter, but that rule has no legal sanction
attached to it, and in arriving at any decision in the selection of a
name, the Chamber is left entirely to its own discretion.

On the above grounds I hold that this Court has no jurisdiction
entitling it to interfere in this matter in the manner asked for by the
plaintiff, and I am further of opinion that the circumstances of the

case are of such a nature as to bring it within the well-established principle that the judiciary cannot properly intervene in matter political and concerning the discharge of executive or political functions except under the express authority of some law or commission in that behalf. The nomination in this case is not a nomination to an office of emolument or an office in which the nominee can be said to have any private right or interest.

The constitution of the Legislative Council and the appointments of its members is entirely in the hands of the Executive branch of the Government, and the authorities seem to show that, except possibly in the case of clearly specified purely ministerial duties imposed upon some public functionary, it would be highly improper on the part of the judiciary and outside its functions to seek to control executive acts.

The choosing of a name by the Chamber of Commerce to be submitted for approval by the proper authority with a view to filling a vacant seat in the Legislative Council is only a step in the performance of an executive act,—the act of making the appointment— and savours so much of the exercise of political functions that on these grounds also I hold that this Court has no jurisdiction in the case before me.

I carefully abstain from expressing any opinion upon the merits of this case or passing judgment in any way upon the conduct of the Chairman and Committee of the Chamber or the validity of the two ballots which took place at the meeting at which the Plaintiff was declared to have been elected, and I only mention the facts in the case so far as is absolutely necessary to explain my reasons for holding that I have no jurisdiction.

The hearing of the motion having been by consent taken as the hearing of the action, there will be judgment for the Defendants.

Costs reserved for further consideration.

Ross as to costs cited the following cases, where although there was no jurisdiction, the Court gave the Defendant his costs

Forbes v. Eden (L. R. 1 Sc. & Div. Ap. 568, 571).

Vavasseur v. Krupp (L. R. 9 Ch. D. 351, 362).

Foster v. Great Western Railway Coy. (L. R. 8 Q. B. D. 25, 31).
Ibid: 515, 517.

And also where the Plaintiff had no legal right.   *Dick v. Yates* (L. R. 18 Ch. D. 76. 84—85, 90—91 and 93).

Adams contended that as the Court had no jurisdiction to hear the case it had no jurisdiction to give costs.

Peacock v. The Queen, (4 C. B. N. S. 264).

(S. C. 27 L. J. C. P. 224).

Brown v. Shaw (L. R. 1 Ex. D. 425). but admitted that these cases had not been followed in *The Great Northern and London and North Western Joint Committee v. Inett* (L. R. 2 Q. B. D. 284)

Annual Practice for 1894, 279.

GATTY J. The cases cited by Plaintiff's Counsel are admitted to be overruled by the last case, and that case followed the rule laid down in the cases cited by Defendants' Counsel that costs ought never to be considered as a penalty or punishment but merely as a necessary consequence of a party having occasioned litigation in which he has failed. There is nothing in the facts too, as far as I know them, that ought to make me deprive the successful party of their costs. I am sorry the Chamber has asked for costs, but as they have, I see no ground for depriving them of costs.

Judgment for Defendants, with costs.

Solicitors for the Plaintiff.—*Hogan & Adams.*

Solicitors for the Defendants.—*Logan & Ross*

SALWATH HANEEM BINTE ALLIE EFFENDI.

v.

HADJEE ABDULLAH BIN HADJEE MOHAMED CASSIM.

INCHE DAUD BIN HADJEE MOHAMED CASSIM AND

HADJEE ARSHAD.

Conveyance by husband to wife—Mohamedan law—Undue influence—Acknowledgment of deed by Mohamedan married woman.

There is no rule of law in the Colony which prevents a Mohamedan husband from conveying property to his wife, and a conveyance from the husband to the wife passes the legal estate in the property conveyed.

The Plaintiff, a Mohamedan married woman, lived with her husband the Defendant A, another wife, and three children of A's of ages from 17 years downwards. The Defendants B & C were brothers of A and had access to the women's quarters of A's house. During A's absence from the Colony from 1878 B had managed A's business, collected his rents, paid his expenses, and supplied Plaintiff with money. A's sons went to a school kept by B who was trustee of certain property for one of A's sons. In 1891, B &

C commenced an action against A, who was the executor of their father's estate, for the administration of such estate; and a judgment for the administration having been made, A was ordered to file his accounts. Having failed to do so an order was made, on the 23rd of November, 1891, on A that he should shew cause why he should not be committed for contempt in not filing his accounts. From the 1st to the 21st of December, 1891, A was seriously ill and unable to attend to business. On the 3rd of December an agreement was entered into between A, the Plaintiff, the other wife, and the three children and B & C whereby the Plaintiff, the other wife, and the children agreed to convey certain land and other property to B & C in consideration of their agreeing not to proceed further with the order of the 23rd of November, 1891. The agreement was signed by the Plaintiff, the other wife, and the three children in A's house in the presence of a clerk of Messrs. *Khory & Brydges* (B & C's Solicitors). The wives and children all gave evidence that they believed the document to be a "kwasa," or trust deed to enable B & C to manage A's affairs in case of his death. On the 8th of December, 1891, the Plaintiff; the other wife, and the children executed conveyances of the land and property mentioned in the agreement of the 3rd of December, and in particular the Plaintiff executed the conveyance which it was sought to set aside in this action. The conveyances were executed in the presence of Mr. Khory, but the wives did not acknowledge the deeds under section 50 of the Conveyancing and Law of Property Ordinance 1886. The wives and children all gave evidence that they believed the deeds were to strengthen the "kwasa" of the 3rd of December. The agreement of the 3rd of December, and the conveyance of the 8th of December, all bore A's signature. The Plaintiff having brought an action to set aside the agreement and conveyance

Held that a confidential relationship existed between the Plaintiff and B & C and that the onus of proof lay on the latter to shew that the Plaintiff fully understood the transaction, executed the agreement and conveyance freely and without being subjected to undue influence, and that in this case B & C not having satisfied the onus, the agreement and conveyance ought to be set aside.

Per Gatty J.—A Mohamedan married woman must convey land acquired by her subsequently to her marriage in accordance with the formalities imposed by the Conveyancing and Law of Property Ordinance 1886, section 50, notwithstanding the provisions of section 27 (XI) of the Mohamedan Marriage Ordinance 1880 (Ordinance V. of 1880).

C. A.
——
GATTY, J.
——
1895.
——
Aug. 8, 10, 15,
22, 23 & 24,
& Oct. 3.

C. A.
——
COX, C. J.
and
LAW, J.
——
1894.
——
Mar. 6, 7, 8,
9 & 12.

THIS was an action to have an agreement dated the 3rd of December, 1891, and made between the Defendant Arshad of the first part, Inche Zainib, the wife of Arshad, Mohamed Noor, son of Arshad, Napea Hanim, son-in-law of Arshad, the Plaintiff, another wife of Arshad, and Abdul Hamid, a son of Arshad, of the second part, and the Defendants, Abdullah, and Daud, of the third part, and a conveyance dated the 8th of December, 1891, made between Arshad of the first part, the Plaintiff of the second part, and Abdullah and Daud of the third part, set aside.

The parties are all Mohamedans. The land comprised in the conveyance originally belonged to one Jemalia, also a wife of Arshad,

C. A.
―――
COX, C. J.
and
LAW, J.
1894
⌣⌣⌣
SALWATH
HANEEM BINTE
ALLIE EFFENDI.
v.
HADJEE ABDUL-
LAH BIN HADJEE
MOHAMED CAS-
SIM,
INCHE DAUD
BIN HADJEE
MOHAMED CAS-
SIM
AND HADJEE
ARSHAD.

On her death he became her administrator, and on the 8th of March, 1882, he conveyed the land in question to the Plaintiff, who was then his wife, in consideration of the sum of $500, which was by the conveyance expressed to have been paid.

The case for the Plaintiff was shortly as follows: At the end of November, 1891, and during the first part of December, Arshad was dangerously ill with fever, and Abdullah, who was (as was also Daud) a half-brother of Arshad, came to the house where Arshad, his two wives, the Plaintiff, and Inche Zainib and his children Mohamed Noor, Napea Hanim, and Abdul Hamid, children of ages from seventeen downwards, were living, representing to the wives and children that as Arshad was very ill it would be better to execute a "kwasa," (trust deed) constituting Daud and himself trustees to look after the family property.   The Plaintiff and Inche Zainib then handed over the title deeds of the property comprised in the abovementioned conveyance, and of other property belonging to themselves and to the children, for the purpose of having the "kwasa" prepared. On the 3rd of December, Abdullah came and told the family that two clerks from Messrs. *Khory and Brydges*, Solicitors, would come with a document for signature and that they were all to sign it.   Thereupon the Plaintiff, Inche Zainib and the three children all signed it believing it to be a "kwasa." On the 8th of December, Abdullah came again to Arshad's house.   Shortly afterwards Mr. Khory, Solicitor, and his two clerks came to the house ; and the conveyance which it was sought to set aside, and also conveyances of other property in the names of the Plaintiff, Inche Zainib, and the three children, were executed in the presence of Mr. Khory and the clerks, the wives and children all believing that such documents were made merely to strengthen the "kwasa." The conveyances executed by the wives were not acknowledged by them under Section 50 of the Conveyancing and Law of Property Ordinance 1886.

The ground of relief as originally set out in the statement of claim was that the agreements and conveyances were obtained by the fraudulent statement of the Defendant Abdullah that they were merely for the purpose of constituting a "kwasa." Subsequently, at the trial before Bovill C. J., two further paragraphs were added to the statement of claim as follows : "The Plaintiff was induced to sign the alleged agreement and the indenture of assignment

C. A.

COX, C. J.
and
LAW. J.

1891.

SALWATE
HANEEM BINTE
ALLIE EFFENDI.
v.
HADJEE ABDUL-
LAH BIN HADJEE
MOHAMED CAS-
SIM.
INCHE DAUD
BIN HADJEE
MOHAMED CAS-
SIM
AND HADJEE
ARSHAD.

under the following circumstances. The third Defendant, Hadjee Arshad, the husband of the Plaintiff, was lying seriously ill and was expected to die, and the first and second Defendants were the brothers of the said Hadjee Arshad and exercised great influence over the Plaintiff. There was no consideration for the alleged agreement and assignment moving from the Defendants to the Plaintiff. The Plaintiff had no independent advice with respect to the alleged agreement and assignment. The alleged agreement and assignment were never properly explained to the Plaintiff.

"The alleged assignment dated the 8th day of December, 1891, has not been acknowledged by the Plaintiff as required by law."

The case for the Defendants was as follows:—

Arshad had been one of the trustees of the will of one Mohamed Cassim, the father of himself, Abdullah and Daud, and an action having been commenced by Abdullah and Daud, against him for the administration of the estate, a decree was made on the 12th of October, 1891, ordering the accounts and enquiries usual in an action for administration to be taken and made. On the 19th of October, 1891, the Defendant was ordered to file his accounts within a month from that date. On the 23rd of November, 1891, Arshad having neglected to file his accounts, an order was made that he should show cause why he should not be punished for disobeying the decree of the 12th of October, 1891 ; the last mentioned order was served on Arshad by Ali, one of Messrs. *Khory and Brydges'* clerks, on the 27th of November ; on the 29th of November, Arshad sent for Ali telling him that he was anxious to compromise the action, and that he and the other members of his family would convey to Abdullah and Daud the property contained in certain title-deeds which he then handed over to Ali. Ali took the title-deeds to Abdullah and read them out to him, whereupon it turned out that the property was not in Arshad's name at all but in the names of his wives and children, it having been conveyed to one or the other of them by Arshad. Ali then took the deeds back to Arshad who said that the property was his and that his wives and children would execute conveyances. An agreement was accordingly drawn by Messrs. *Khory and Brydges* and a draft of it left, on the 30th of November, with Arshad. On the 3rd of December, Ali and Palonjee (another clerk of Messrs. *Khory and Brydges*) went to Arshad's house.

Arshad appeared to be in a good state of health. The agreement was
explained by Palonjee to the parties of the first and second parts and
duly signed by them in duplicate. Subsequently the duplicate agreement after being signed by Abdullah and Daud was handed back
to Arshad. On the 8th of December, Mr. Khory, Palonjee, and Ali
again went to Arshad's house with the conveyance which was now
sought to be set aside, and other conveyanc·s of other property for
execution by Arshad, the Plaintiff, Inche Zainib, and the children.
The conveyances were explained and executed by the part'es. On the
10th Mr. Khory and his clerks again called at Arshad's house and
procured the execution by Arshad of an indenture of release from
Abdullah and Daud to Arshad, it having been previously executed by
Abdullah and Daud. On the 6th, the 8th, and the 10th, Arshad had
appeared to Mr. Khory to be in good health. The release, which bore
the date of the 8th of December, 1891, and was expressed to be made
between Abdullah and Daud of the one part, and Arshad of the other
part, recited the will of Mohamed Cassim and the proceedings in the
action stated above : and, further, that Arshad had never yet rendered
any account, and that there was then due from him, as executor of
the will of Mohamed Cassim, to Abdullah and Daud, the sum of
$37.480.77¼, as Arshad admitted ; and that Arshad had requested
Abdullah and Daud not to proceed further under the order of the 23rd
of November, 1891, or generally in the said suit, and to execute to him
such release as was thereinafter contained. That the said Hadjee
Abdullah and Inche Daud agreed so to do, on condition that the said
Hadjee Mohamed Arshad should, in consideration thereof, assign
and transfer to them the several lands, tenements, hereditaments, and
ships, specified in the second schedule thereunder written and should
also procure the assignment thereof to them by the several persons to
whom he had previously assigned the same respectively. And that
such lands had been assigned and transferred to Abdullah and Daud,
as tenants in common, by Arshad, and by the said several persons by
indentures bearing the same date as the indentures of release but
executed before them. The deed then contained a release by Abdullah
and Daud of Arshad of the sum of $37,480.77¼ and from all actions,
claims, and demands, whatsoever, for, or in respect, or on account
of the estate of Mohamed Cassim. The lands and ships mentioned in
the second schedule to the said release comprised the property of which

C. A.

COX, C. J.
and
LAW, J.

1894.

SALWATH
HANEEM BINTE
ALLIE EFFENDI.
v.
HADJEE ABDUL-
LAH BIN HADJEE
MOHAMED CAS-
SIM,
INCHE DAUD
BIN HADJEE
MOHAMED CAS-
SIM
AND HADJEE
ARSHAD.

C. A.
COX, C. J.
and
LAW, J.

1894.

SALWATH
HANNEM BINTE
ALLIE EFFENDI
v.
HADJEE ABDUL-
LAH BIN HADJEE
MOHAMED CAS-
SIM,
INCHE DAUD
BIN HADJEE
MOHAMED CAS-
SIM
AND HADJEE
ARSHAD.

conveyances had been previously executed by the wives and children of Arshad on the 8th of December.

The action was originally heard before Bovill C. J. on the 15th. 16th, 21st, 22nd, 23rd. and 28th of February, and on the 1st and 16th of March, 1893, and a considerable mass of evidence was taken, including the evidence of Dr. Galloway, who deposed that he attended Arshad from the 1st to the 21st of December, 1891. He was in bed at that time and dangerously ill and during that period he could not have been in a state to transact business of his own volition. and although he might have signed the documents, Dr. Galloway doubted whether he could have exercised any judgment as to what he was doing.

On the hearing before Bovill C. J. *Drew* and *Koek* appeared for the Plaintiff. and *Nanson* and *Brydges* for the Defendants Abdullah and Daud.

At that time Arshad had not been made a party. After hearing the arguments of Counsel. Bovill C. J. died without giving his judgment.

Subsequently Arshad was joined as a Defendant to the action but he did not enter an appearance.

The matter then came on before Gatty J. on the 8th of August, 1893, and was heard on that day and on the 10th, 15th, 22nd, 23rd. and 24th of August.

Napier (*Koek* with him) appeared for the Plaintiff, and *Nanson* for the Defendants Abdullah and Daud. Nearly all the witnesses who had given evidence at the former trial were recalled ; and in addition Mr. Khory, who had been in Europe during the former trial. was examined as a witness ; but as the subsequent case was more fully argued in the Court of Appeal, it is not necessary to set out the arguments of Counsel or the cases cited by them.

Judgment was delivered on the 3rd of October, 1893.

GATTY, J.

(After having stated the nature and grounds of the Plaintiff's claim and the grounds of the defence.) During the progress of the case Arshad has been added as a Defendant, and the pleadings have been so far amended that the Plaintiff has been allowed to set up a case of undue influence. The case has occupied a very long time. There was a mass of evidence taken before the late Chief Justice, and nearly all the witnesses called before the late Chief Justice have been further examined in this Court, and what I have to do is to come to a conclusion whether or not any of the grounds of relief have been proved by the Plaintiff so as to allow her to have this deed set aside so far as she goes.

One remarkable fact in the case is that the Plaintiff, who was the wife of Arshad, never really appeared upon the scene at all until the execution of these two instruments. There was no history given of what took place to induce her to sign either of these documents, except the history which she herself gave that she was induced to sign them by the representations made by the Defendant Abdullah, who was a brother of her husband. She was a Turkish woman living in the privacy which was usual amongst these people, and there were but two persons who had access apparently to the women's rooms, the man Arshad, her husband, and the Defendant Abdullah who was her husband's brother ; and he is the person who eventually took the benefit of this conveyance, (if benefit could be legally claimed,) of the 8th of December, 1891.

Those being the circumstances of the case I have come to the conclusion that this was one of those cases in which an undue influence was certainly likely to be exercised. It became, therefore, the duty of the person who took the benefit of the deed to show that the transaction was one made in good faith, and one which could be supported by the principles which govern cases of undue influence.

The question of undue influence is sought to be thrown out of the case by an allegation that the deed which the wife took from her husband was a purely voluntary one. And although that deed, which was dated 1882, stated a consideration of $500, a substantial consideration, and although the woman swore that she paid it, and her husband said so too, yet I am asked—because there was some other transaction as to the property of Arshad's son, or what was alleged to be the property of Arshad's son—to hold that it was unlikely that any consideration should have passed, to hold as a fact that there never was any payment of $500 in 1882, and that, therefore, it was a voluntary conveyance, and that the Plaintiff could not have conveyed anything on the 8th of December, 1891. I should not be at all justified in doing so on the evidence. Quite apart from the question of this document I hold, so far as I am able to judge from the facts, that this was a true statement of consideration. There was nothing to show

C. A.

COX, C. J.
and
LAW, J.

1894.

SALWATH
HANEEM BINTE
ALLIE EFFENDI.
r.
HADJEE ABDUL-
LAH BIN HADJEE
MOHAMED CAS-
SIN,
INCHE DAUP
BIN HADJEE
MOHAMED CAS-
SIN
AND HADJEE
ARSHAD.

C. A.

COX, C. J.
and
LAW, J.

1894.

SALWATH
HANEEM BINTE
ALLIB EFFENDI.
v.
HADJEE ABDUL-
LAH BIN HADJEE
MOHAMED CAS-
SIM,
INCHE DAUD
BIN HADJEE
MOHAMED CAS-
SIM
AND HADJEE
ARSHAD.

that it was not, it was sworn to positively by the Plaintiff and her husband; and if I were to set aside a deed some eight or nine years old on the ground that the consideration was not properly stated I think I should be bound to insist upon a great deal more evidence than has been produced or even suggested to me. to come to the conclusion that that document was a voluntary deed. Therefore I hold, in the first place, that the deed of 1882 between Arshad and his wife was for a valuable consideration.

It was also argued that apart from the fact that there was no money consideration for the deed of the 8th of December, 1891. there was really consideration because there was a forbearance to do something, but it was not a forbearance to do something which operated in favour of the Plaintiff, it operated in favour of Arshad; and, as I hold, rendered it a deed which was a voluntary one. This being a voluntary deed as I hold it to be, and this agreement being a voluntary agreement, the question arose whether or not this was a *bona fide* transaction. I hold that it was not.

It was clearly a case in which it was absolutely necessary there should be the intervention of some disinterested person on behalf of the Plaintiff, and on that ground alone I think this transaction cannot be supported. Here was a wife, living with her husband, under her husband's influence, and the other party to the deed was a brother-in-law who had access to the premises; and if ever there was a case in which it was desirable and necessary that the woman should have independent and proper advice before she entered into any such contract as this I think this is such a case. There were other considerations which only went to build up the case and to make it still more necessary that the Plaintiff should have had full knowledge of what she was doing. This case comes very near being one of that class of cases which one finds in the books, where people had acted under fear, because there was a threat of proceedings against her husband, a threat that practically amounted to a threat of imprisonment; and it was extremely likely to have influenced her if that threat was brought to her knowledge. I think it was Defendants' own fault if they did not see to it that at the time this transaction was carried out the Plaintiff had independent and separate advice, and on that ground alone I come to the conclusion that this transaction ought not to stand. I find that was a ground on which there was ample authority for setting aside such a transaction, [see the notes to *Huguenin v. Baseley*, White and Tudor's Leading Cases in Equity vol. II (5th edit:) p. 547.]

A point of law was raised as to which I perhaps, ought to express some opinion, because if the contention on the one side is right it disposes of the whole case at once. The point of law was that the conveyance was a document which under the law of Conveyancing as applied to this Colony ought to have been acknowledged before a judge, and I hold that it ought so to have been acknowledged. I think that when the Indian Act was repealed by the Conveyancing Ordinance VI. of 1886 all methods of conveyancing by a married woman were swept away and new ones instituted, and I find that according to section 50 all deeds executed by married women must be acknowledged before the judge. I think the effect of the repeal of the Indian Act was this, that from the moment it was repealed no married woman could convey under that Act, and therefore the authority for married women conveying came from section 50 of the Conveyancing Ordinance, and that although it may have been a slip on the part of the drafters of this Ordinance that Mohammedan women were not expressly exempted from the formalities required by this new law, yet I think it was quite likely that the Legislature should have intended that Mohammedan women should not be exempted from these formalities. I think this is a case which shows that the latter would have been by far the wiser course to have taken, and I hold that, whether it was intended or not, the Legislature made it necessary by section 50 as it now stands that all deeds executed by married women should be acknowledged. It was argued on behalf of the defendants (other than Arshad) that Arshad's influence, even if there was undue influence, could not affect them. I find that, on page 586 of the 2nd volume of White and Tudor's Leading Cases there are cases in which it was clearly laid down that the Court would interfere although the person who received the benefit of the deed might not have been a party to the undue influence. And therefore I have not the least doubt that if the undue influence, which I think in this case must have existed, was the influence only of the defendant Arshad, still the brothers could not take advantage of it. It ought to have been those defendants' first care, and they should have insisted upon it, that there should have been a separate adviser given to the plaintiff in

C. A.
___
COX, C. J
and
LAW, J
1894.
~~~
SALWATH
HANEEM BINTE
ALLIE EFFENDI.
v.
HADJEE ABDUL-
LAH BIN HADJEE
MOHAMED CAS-
SIM.
INCHE DAUD
BIN HADJEE
MOHAMED CAS-
SIM
AND HADJEE
ARSHAD.

C. A.
COX, C. J.
and
LAW. J.
1894.

SALWATH
HANEEM BINTE
ALLIE EYYENDI.
v.
HADJEE ABDUL-
LAH BIN HADJEE
MOHAMED CAS-
SIM.
INCHE DAUD
BIN HADJEE
MOHAMED CAS-
SIM
AND HADJEE
ARSHAD.

this action. There was evidence no doubt that she heard the deed read over, and the clerks in Mr. Khory's office, and Mr. Khory himself, stated that it was read over to her and that she appeared to understand it; but that was not enough. It was read to her through an interpreter, and it is extremely difficult for either Mr. Khory or his clerks to come here and say with any certainty or positiveness that she had a sufficient knowledge of what she was doing merely by having a deed read over to her or by hearing what was said on that occasion. Mr. Khory admitted that he did not enter into any lengthy conversation with her himself. It would be unsafe, therefore, for me to come to a conclusion that she heard enough to put her on her guard and to enable her to come to a proper conclusion herself. Besides, it came too late. The time when she ought to have had that advice was at the beginning, before she gave up these deeds; before these deeds were prepared. The influence had been at work already, if there was undue influence, and the time when she most wanted advice was before these documents were given up and before instructions were given by her husband to Messrs. Khory and Brydges to prepare the deeds. If the defendants suffer by these deeds being set aside it is entirely the fault of their solicitors. I think that in a community like this where there are people speaking foreign languages, and in which everything has to be explained through an interpreter, it is incumbent upon every practitioner to see that where a person has need of independent advice that that independent advice is obtained on behalf of the person whose decision is required. This agreement ought never to have been drawn up until Messrs. Khory and Brydges had insisted upon a solicitor being employed in the interests of the married woman, and then it is probable I should never have had this case in Court. I give judgment in favour of the plaintiff, holding that this is essentially a case in which the relief of the Court is properly sought to set aside a transaction which, on the face of it, required a great deal more care than has apparently been bestowed upon it.

GATTY J. on being asked for the reasons for his judgment referred to his judgment as set out above with the following addition. "I ought perhaps however to add what I stated orally in Court and which appears to have escaped the short-hand writers' notice viz. that while I did not find for or against the Plaintiff on the issue raised in the pleadings as to the particular fraud alleged by the Plaintiff, I held that it was not in my opinion at all unlikely or incompatible with the evidence before the Court that the Plaintiff had been deceived in the manner alleged into believing that what she was signing was a power of Attorney."

The Defendants Abdullah and Daud appealed from *Gatty J.'s* judgment.

The appeal was heard before *Cox, C. J. and Law J.* on the 6th, 7th, 8th, 9th, and 12th of March, 1894.

Nanson, for the Defendants Abdullah and Daud.

(1.) The conveyance of the 8th of March, 1882, from Arshad to the Plaintiff, was inoperative, being a conveyance by a husband to his wife.

Beard v. Beard, (3 Atk. 72.)

[*COX, C. J.* How is that law within this Colony ?]

It is one of the rules of English law which are in force in the Colony. The rule is not modified by Mohamedan law which by section 27 (II) of the Mohamedan Marriage Ordinance 1880, (Ordinance V of 1880) is only to be recognised by the Courts of the Colony so far as is expressly enacted in section 27 of that Ordinance.

(2) It was unnecessary that the Plaintiff should acknowledge the deed of the 8th of December, 1891, under section 50 of the Conveyancing and Law of Property Ordinance 1886. Under the Mohamedan Marriage Ordinance 1880 section 27 (XI) the property was her separate estate and she could dispose of it by simple deed.

Taylor v. Meads (4 De G. J. & S. 597 ; 34. L. J. Ch. 203.)

In re Drummond and Davie's Contract, [L. R. (1891), 1 Ch. 524.]

Dart on the Law of Vendors and Purchasers, (6th Ed. Vol. II p. 643.)

The concurrence of her husband is expressly stated to be unnecessary; and where the concurrence of the husband is unnecessary a married woman need not acknowledge a conveyance.

(3) As to the general question the Plaintiff and her witnesses have sworn to actual fraud, and to enable her to succeed the Court must believe that the fraud was practised upon her. The judgment can only be *secundum allegata et probata*. The Court cannot upset the agreement and conveyance on the ground of undue influence on the part of Arshad, for the Plaintiff has sworn that such undue

C. A.

COX, C. J. and LAW, J.

1894

SALWATH HANEEM BISTE ALLIE EFFENDI. *v.* HADJEE ABDULLAH BIN HADJEE MOHAMED CASSIM, INCHE DAUD BIN HADJEE MOHAMED CASSIM AND HADJEE ARSHAD.

C. A.

COX, C. J.
and
LAW, J.

1894.

SALWATH
HANEEM BINTS
ALLIE EFFENDI.
v.
HADJEE ABDUL-
LAH BIN HADJEE
MOHAMED CAS-
SIM,
INCHE DAUD
BIN HADJEE
MOHAMED CAS-
SIM
AND HADJEE
ARSHAD.

influence did not exist.

Gatty, J., said the Plaintiff ought to have been represented by a separate solicitor but what advice could such solicitor have given? He could only have said, "Well, are you willing to make this sacrifice for your husband."

A person who signs a contract cannot be heard to say he did not understand the contents.

Ismail bin Savoosah v. Hadjee Ismail (4, Kyshe 453.)

In this case there was a valuable consideration for the agreement and conveyance—the forbearance by Abdullah and Daud to proceed against Arshad.

Attwood v. ———— (1 Russ 353.)

Crears v. Hunter, (L. R. 19 Q. B. D. 341.)

Smith v. Algar, (1, B. & Ad. 603.)

Payne v. Wilson, (7, B. & C. 423.)

Callisher v. Bischoffsheim, (L. R. 5 Q. B. 449.)

Miles v. New Zealand Alford Estate Coy. (L. R. 32 C. D. 266.)

The Court should look upon a family arrangement of this kind with favour and not with suspicion. The Court will not presume a husband to have exercised undue influence over his wife.

Grigby v. Cox, (1 Ves Sen. 517.)

Field v. Sowle, (4 Russ. 112.)

Brydges followed on the same side. On the last point, that the relation of husband and wife is not a confidential one so that undue influence is presumed, he cited the following cases :

Nedby v. Nedby, (5 De. G. & S. 377.)

Blackie v. Clark, (15 Beav. 595.)

Hunter v. Atkins, (3 Myl. & K. 113.)

Beanland v. Bradley, (2 Sm. & Giff. 339.)

There is no confidential relationship between Abdullah and Daud and the Plaintiff and therefore the onus of proof is on the Plaintiff.

The Plaintiff's case here is fraud and even if she had had separate advice that would not have prevented her from alleging and proving this fraud.

Moxon v. Payne (L. R. 8 Ch. App. 881).

Gatty, J., has held that the Mohamedan Marriage Ordinance in so far as it obviated the necessity of acknowledgment by a married woman of a deed is repealed by section 50 of the Conveyancing

and Law of Property Ordinance 1886; but a later general law does
not abrogate an earlier special one. *Maxwell* on Statutes (1st edit.)
p. 157.

C. A.

COX, C. J.
and
LAW, J.

1894.

SALWATH
HANEEM BINTE
ALLIE EFFENDI.
v.
HADJEE ABDUL-
LAN BIN HADJEE
MOHAMED CAS-
SIM,
INCHE DAUD
BIN HADJEE
MOHAMED CAS-
SIM
AND HAIJEE
ARSHAD.

Napier (*Drew* and *Koek* with him) for the Plaintiff.

(1) The English rule preventing   husband conveying land to his
wife does not apply to this Colony. *Sherifa Fatimah v. Fleury* (1 S. S.
L. R. 49).   Certainly it does not apply between Mohamedans, for a
marriage between them is essentially different from that between
Christians.

Hawah v. Daud (Leicester's Straits Reports 253.)

Chulas v. Kolson (Leicester's Straits Reports 462.)

Haleemah v. Bradford, (Leicester's Straits Reports 383).

As to Chinese marriages, *Lim Chooi Hoon v. Chok Yoon Guan*
(1 S. S. L. R. 72).

(2) *Taylor v. Meads* (*v.* supra) only applies to the equitable
estate of a married woman; in England before the Married Women's
Property Act. 1882 if land were granted to a married woman without
the intervention of trustees, for her separate use, in order to pass the
legal estate her husband must join and she must acknowledge her
deed.

MacQueen on Husband and Wife 3rd edit. 303.

So here although land conveyed to a Mohamedan married
woman before the Act of 1880 belonged to her as her separate estate
yet to make a valid conveyance she had to acknowledge her deed.

Chulas v. Kolson (*v.* supra.)

Kader Meydin v. Shatomah (Leicester's Straits Reports 260.)

Fatimah v. Armootah Pullay (4 Kyshe 225.)

This case is governed by the Mohamedan Marriage Ordinance
1880 sec. 27 (XI) and since this section does not do away with the
necessity of acknowledgment by a married woman it is still required.

(3)   The facts shew that Abdullah and Daud were in a fiduciary
relation to the Plaintiff and therefore the onus is on them to prove
that she understood the transaction and entered into it freely.
He cited

Huguenin v. Baseley (2 White and Tudor's Leading Cases in Equity
5th Edit. 547.)

Cooke v. Lamotte (15 Beav. 234.)

Hoghton v. Hoghton (15 Beav. 278.)

C. A.

COX, C. J.
and
LAW, J.

1894.

SALWATH
HANEEM BINTE
ALLIE EFFENDI.
v.
HADJEE ABDUL-
LAH BIN HADJEE
MOHAMED CAS-
SIM,
INCHE DAUD
BIN HADJEE
MOHAMED CAS-
SIM
AND HADJEE
ARSHAD.

Allcard v. Skinner (L. R. 36 C. D. 145.)

Morley v. Laughnan [L. R. (1893) 1 Ch. 736.]

If the Court should come to the conclusion that Abdullah and Daud were not in a fiduciary position to the Plaintiff, yet as Arshad was in a fiduciary relation to her and he took the benefit of the consideration, still the onus will lie on Abdullah and Daud.

Maitland v. Irving (15 Sim. 437).

Sercombe v. Sanders (34 Beav. 382).

Berdoe v. Dawson, (34 Beav. 603).

Kempson v. Ashbee (L. R. 10 Ch. App. 15).

A husband is in a fiduciary relation towards his wife.

Parfitt v. Lawless (L. R. 2 P. & D. 462) see per Lord Penzance on p. 468.

Corbett v. Brock (20 Beav. 524).

The Court will not support the transaction as a family arrangement. The parties were not on equal terms and it is clear that the Plaintiff had not all information given her, for the accounts were never gone into until after the conveyance had been signed. *see* notes to *Stapilton v. Stapilton* (White and Tudor's Leading Cases in Equity Vol. II. (5th Edit). p. 838).

Nanson was heard in reply.

C. A. V.

Judgment was delivered on the 2nd of April, 1894.

COX, C. J.

This was an appeal from a judgment of Mr. *Justice Gatty* given in a suit instituted by the respondent, Salwath Haneem, a married woman against the appellants, in which the respondent asked the Court to set aside as fraudulent and void, *1st*, an agreement made by her on the 3rd of December, 1891, with the appellants respecting a house and land in Campong Java Road, and *2nd*, a conveyance of the said house and land executed by her in favour of the appellants on the 8th of December, 1891. In the statement of Claim the Plaintiff averred that she had been induced to sign the agreement and indenture of conveyance by a false statement that the two documents were only for appointing the Defendants as trustees of the property. The Plaintiff further alleged that her husband Arshad—then seriously ill—exercised great influence over her; that there was no consideration for the agreement and assignment, and that the said documents were not properly explained to her. The Defendants in their statement of Defence denied that the execution of the document had been induced by fraud. They averred that the deeds had been fully and accurately explained to the Plaintiff and that there had been valuable consideration *i. e.* an agreement by the Defendants not to proceed further in an action entered by them against the Plaintiff's husband, Hadjee Arshad. as executor of their father's will, and to grant to the said Hadjee Arshad a release from all claims and demands. which agreement had been duly performed by the Defendants. The case first came before the late Chief Justice, Sir *Elliot Bovill*. but judgment had not been given when he died, and it was then reheard by Mr. *Justice Gatty*. By consent, the evidence taken before Sir Elliot Bovill was put in ; further evidence was also taken, Hadjee Arshad, the Plaintiff's husband was added as a Defendant in the cause and on the 3rd of October, 1893. Mr. *Justice Gatty* gave judgment in favour of the Plaintff. The agreement and conveyance of December, 1891, were pronounced void and not binding on the Plaintiff, she recovered possession of the house and land, an account of the rents received by the Defendants was ordered to be taken and the Defendants were further ordered to deliver the title deeds, etc. Against this judgment, the Defendants have appealed.

Before dealing with the grounds of appeal I think it is necessary to state the general facts of the case as they appear to me to be proved by the evidence.

The Defendants, Hadjee Abdullah and Daud, are the younger brothers of Hadjee Arshad, the Plaintiff's husband. Hadjee Arshad was the executor of his father's will and as such administered the estate. He went to Arabia in 1878 and apparently returned to Singapore only in 1889. During his absence, the father's estate was managed by Hadjee Abdullah who also looked after Hadjee Arshad's property. Hadjee Abdullah said in his evidence "I did manage Hadjee Arshad's business from 1878 to 1889. During that period he was sometimes away. If at these times Salwath (Plaintiff) wanted money I would see that she got it. Hadjee Arshad used to get me to look after the business and the family from 1878 to 1889. I was collecting all Hadjee Arshad's rents and paying out for his expenses." All the parties were then on intimate terms ; Abdullah and Daud were frequently in their brother's house and would go in and out of

C. A.
COX, C. J.
and
LAW, J.
1894.

SALWATH HANEEM BINTE ALLIE EFFENDI.
v.
HADJEE ABDULLAH BIN HADJEE MOHAMED CASSIM.
INCHE DAUD BIN HADJEE MOHAMED CASSIM
AND HADJEE ARSHAD.

the women's quarters of the house. Arshad's sons went to school in Abdullah's house and also frequently went to his place to play with their relatives. Abdullah was trustee of a house in Beach Road for one of the sons. In 1891 difficulties arose between the brothers, and Abdullah and Daud entered an action against Arshad, claiming accounts of his administration as executor of their father's estate. Arshad did not defend the actions. He says that Abdullah had induced him not to appear, and on the 19th of October, 1891, he was ordered to file his accounts. Arshad did not file his accounts, and on November the 23rd 1891, Abdullah and Daud obtained a rule calling upon him to show cause why he should not be committed for contempt. The rule was served on Arshad on the 27th of November, and on the 3rd, and 8th of December, 1891, the agreement and conveyance which the Plaintiff seeks to have set aside were signed. The agreement of the 3rd of December, 1891. was made between the Defendants Abdullah and Daud on the one side, and on the other side 1st the Plaintiff Salwath Haneem. 2nd Inche Zainab, another wife of Arshad, 3rd Napeah Haneem, the daughter of the Plaintiff, then about 14 years old: 4th Mohamed Noor. son of Arshad, about 17 years old; 5th Abdul Hamid, another son of Arshad 14 years old; 6th Hadjee Arshad himself. The deed, after a reference to the decree made against Arshad in the administration suit and the order calling upon him to show why he should not be punished for disobeying the decree, states that Arshad and the parties named above had requested Abdullah and Daud not to proceed further on the order of the 23rd of November, 1891. and then follows the agreement :—
" In consideration of Abdullah and Daud agreeing not to proceed further under the said order, the said parties covenant and agree to assign and convey to Abdullah and Daud all the lands, tenements, and steamships comprised in the instruments set forth in the schedule." The documents referred to in the schedule are the title deeds of 1st, the house and land belonging to Salwath ; 2nd another house belonging to Zainab; 3rd a house belonging to Napeah, and 4th and 5th the steam launches *Pathol Khir* and *Suka Hati*. belonging to Mohamed Noor, and Abdul Hamid. The effect of this transaction therefore is that the two women, Salwath and Inche Zainab, and the three infants Napeah, Abdul Hamid and Mohamed Noor, make over property to the Defendants, the only consideration for the assignment being the

agreement of the Defendants not to proceed further against Hadjee Arshad under the order of the 23rd of November, 1891. The indenture of the 8th of December, 1891, is made between the Defendants on the one side and Salwath and Hadjee Arshad on the other, and witnesses a conveyance by them to the Defendants of the house and land belonging to Salwath, in execution of the promise made by her in the agreement of the 3rd of December. It is now necessary to examine under what circumstances the above instruments were executed by the Plaintiff. Her account of the transaction is as follows : She says that at the time her husband, Hadjee Arshad, was very ill, the Defendants had come to see him several times, and on one of these visits the Defendant Abdullah told her "my brother is very ill, we had better make a "kwasa" (power of attorney) to look after the property." She agreed to this, and he said that a person would come to get her signature. Shortly after, a lawyer's clerk came with a document which she was asked to sign. She did so, and her daughter, Napeah, as well as the other wife of Arshad, Inche Zainab, and the boys Abdul Hamid and Mohamed Noor also signed. The document was not explained to them and she executed it believing it to be, what Abdullah had said, a power of attorney or "kwasa." The document is the agreement of December the 3rd, 1891. Abdullah also told her that a lawyer would bring for her signature another paper which was one confirming the first so that no one could disturb it. Afterwards, a lawyer came with a document which was not explained to her and which she also signed believing it to be a "kwasa." Inche Zainab, Napeah, Abdul Hamid, and Mohamed Noor all gave similar evidence corroborating the Plaintiff's statement that the agreement of the 3rd of December, 1891, was represented to them as being a "kwasa" or power of attorney and they executed it as such. All those allegations are denied by the Defendants who swear and have called other witnesses to prove that the agreement of the 3rd of December, 1891, and the indenture of the 8th of December had been fully explained to the parties who signed them, well knowing what they were doing.

In dealing with these issues of fact we must first ascertain on which side lies the burden of proof in this case. It is a well recognised doctrine of equity that when a confidential relationship has existed between two persons and one of them has obtained from the

C. A.

COX, C. J.
and
LAW, J.

1894.

SALWATH
HANEEM BINTE
ALLIE EFFENDI.
v.
HADJEE ABDUL-
LAH BIN HADJEE
MOHAMED CAS-
SIM,
INCHE DAUD
BIN HADJEE
MOHAMED CAS-
SIM
AND HADJEE
ARSHAD.

C. A.

COX, C. J.
and
LAW. J.

1891.

SALWATH
HANEEM BINTE
ALLIE EFFENDI.
v.
HADJEE ABDUL-
LAH BIN HADJEE
MOHAMED CAS-
SIM.
INCHE DAUD
BIN HADJEE
MOHAMED CAS-
SIM
AND HADJEE
ARSHAD.

other a conveyance of property or other advantage for which he has given no consideration, then it is for such party, if he claims the benefit of the transaction, to prove that it was a righteous and proper transaction. And accordingly such party must show that the deed he sets up as embodying the transaction was fully understood by the person who executed it, and that such person executed it freely and without being subjected to undue influence. It was contended for the Defendants that the rule does not apply in this case, because there was no "confidential relationship" between the Plaintiff and the Defendants. Upon the evidence I am satisfied that there was such a relationship between the parties. The Defendants are the brothers-in-law of the Plaintiff. When her husband, Arshad, was absent from the Colony from 1878 to 1889, Abdullah managed his business. collected his rents, paid his expenses, supplied her with money for her wants, in fact acted as her husband's representative. Now at the beginning of December, 1891, Arshad was not absent, but he was lying on his bed dangerously ill and unable to attend to business. This point has been disputed, but the evidence of Dr. Galloway leaves no doubt in my mind upon it. Dr. Galloway says :—" I attended Arshad from 1st to 21st December, 1891. On the 1st of December he was delirious, and in a high state of fever. I saw him daily, I can say that from the 1st to the 10th he was delirious, he was in bed all that time and dangerously ill. He cannot have been in a state to transact business. He might have signed documents. I doubt whether he could have exercised any judgment as to what he was doing." Arshad being in the condition thus described by Dr. Galloway, the Plaintiff Salwath, the other wife Zainab and the children must have looked upon Abdullah as the representative of their husband and father, as the head of the family from whom they could expect advice and protection. Under such circumstances, his influence over them must have been necessarily great ; whatever he said they would be inclined to believe and whatever he suggested or asked they would be inclined to do. I think it clear therefore, upon the facts of the case, that there was between the parties a confidential relationship. But it was further urged for the Defendants that the rule referred to above by which the *onus probandi* is laid on the party setting up the conveyance, is applicable only when the conveyance is a voluntary one, while here there was consideration *i. e.* the promise by the Defendant not to proceed

C. A.

COX, C. J.
and
LAW, J.

1894.

SALWATH
HAKEEM BINTE
ALLIE EFFENDI.
v.
HADJEE ABDUL-
LAH BIN HADJEE
MOHAMED CAS-
SIM,
INCHE DAUD
BIN HADJEE
MOHAMED CAS-
SIM
AND HADJEE
ARSHAD.

further against Arshad and the release which they eventually gave him. It is true that *Huguenin and Baseley* (2 White and Tudor's L. C. 547) and similar cases in which the rule referred to was first acted upon in the Courts of Equity, were generally cases of voluntary conveyance, in the nature of gifts. But in some and more recent decisions the rule was followed although the conveyance proceeded on some consideration analogous to what is set up in this case. Thus in *Sercombe v. Sanders* (34 Beav. 382), the Plaintiff had execut- ed a mortgage soon after he came of age as security for a debt due by his elder brother. The deed was set aside because it was not shewn that the Plaintiff at the time was emancipated from control and had separate advice. In *Berdoe v. Dawson* (34 Beav. 603), the Plaintiff had given security for his father who was pressed for payment by a creditor. The deed was set aside because, the burden of proof lying on the Defendants, they had failed to prove that the Plaintiff knew the true nature of the transaction and that there had been no undue influence. A similar decision was arrived at in *Kempson v. Ashbee* (L. R. 10 Ch. App. 15) and upon those authorities it must be held that the burden of proof in this case lies on the Defendants. This conclusion is also supported by the Evidence Ordinance 1898 section 111 which provides that " when there is a question as to the good faith of a transaction between parties one of whom stands to the other in a position of active confidence, the bur- den of proving the good faith of the transaction is on the party who is in a position of active confidence." The question therefore which we have to decide is, have the Defendants proved that the transactions challenged by the Plaintiff were right and proper transactions, that she understood fully what she was doing, and further that she acted freely and without being subject to undue influence or pressure. I must say that the story told by the Plaintiff and the other members of the family, confirmed as it is by the evidence of Dr. Galloway, upon the important fact that Arshad was then dangerously ill, appears to me to be more probable than what the Defendants have stated. But it is not necessary to find that the charges of fraud and misrepresentation have been proved. It is sufficient to say that the Defendants have failed to show to my satisfaction that when the Plaintiff signed the agreement of the 3rd of December, 1891, she knew and understood that she was signing away

C. A.
COX, C. J.
and
LAW, J.
1894.

SALWATH
HANEEM BINTE
ALLIE EFFENDI.
v.
HADJEE ABDUL-
LAH BIN HADJEE
MOHAMED CAS-
SIM,
INCHE DAUD
BIN HADJEE
MOHAMED CAS-
SIM
AND HADJEE
ARSHAD.

her property as the Defendants contend.   With regard to the conveyance of the 8th of December, 1891, the Defendants' case is somewhat
different.   This document was signed in the presence of Mr. Khory,
a Solicitor of this Court, who was satisfied that the parties understood
what they were doing.   But as Mr. Khory was not able to communi-
cate directly with the parties, and had to use an interpreter, his
evidence *per se* cannot be taken as conclusive on the question.   It is
still necessary to fall back upon the evidence of the person who acted
as interpreter, and that evidence does not satisfy me that the Plaintiff
fully and clearly understood what was the nature and effect of the
document she was signing.   Even if the evidence could be looked
upon as shewing that the Plaintiff knew and understood what she
was doing, it could not be looked upon as proving the other fact which
the Defendants have to make out, *viz.* : that these instruments were
executed by her freely and without being subjected to any undue
influence.   For these reasons I am of opinion that the Court below
was right in holding the agreement of the 3rd of December, 1891, and
the conveyance of the 8th of December, 1891, void, and not binding
upon the Plaintiff.

But we have still to consider another point raised by Defendants.
The house and land conveyed to them by the indenture of December
the 8th, 1891, had been conveyed to the Plaintiff by her husband by
deed of the 8th of March, 1882.   It is urged for the Defendants that
such a conveyance by husband to wife was void according to the common
law of England which applied here, accordingly that nothing passed to
the wife by the conveyance, the legal estate remaining vested in Arshad,
and that by the indenture of the 8th of December, 1891, to which
Arshad was a party, the legal estate was conveyed by him and passed
to the Defendants.   Our attention was also called to the Mahomedan Marriage Ordinance of 1880, section 27 (XVI) as supporting this
contention.   It seems clear that by the law of England before the
Conveyancing Act 1881, and the Married Women's Property Act, 1882,
the wife was incapable of contracting with her husband and therefore
the husband could not make a valid conveyance to her.   Equity, however
recognised such contracts and gave effect to them by holding the
husband in whom the legal estate remained as trustee for the wife.
Assuming, therefore, that the above rule of the common law of
England applied to this Colony in 1882 the result would appear to be

that after the conveyance of 1882, Arshad held as trustee for the Plaintiff, and when he conveyed to the Defendants in 1891 the estate passed subject to the trust of which the Defendants had notice. But I am of opinion that the rule referred to does not apply here in the case of a Mahomedan woman. It is founded on the fiction that husband and wife are one person in law, and the judgment of Sir Benson Maxwell in *Chulas v. Kolson* (Leicester's Straits Reports 4C2) shews conclusively that all such rules of English law of marriage are not applicable to non-Christian marriages. Still less could such a rule be acted upon since the passing of the Mahomedan Marriage Ordinance V of 1880. which provides that a Mahomedan married woman may contract, acquire, and hold separate property and dispose of it without the consent of her husband. For the above reasons I am of opinion that the judgment appealed from is right and should be affirmed. It is not necessary for me to express an opinion on the other questions which have been discussed in the case. Nothing more can be said on the subject until the other cases in which the conveyances made to the Defendants by Zainab and other members of the family are challenged, have been decided upon. When those cases have been disposed of, the Defendants may move the Court for such orders as may be necessary to prevent injustice. The appeal should be dismissed with costs.

LAW J. I concur.

Solicitor for the Plaintiff.—*E. R. Koek.*

Solicitors for the Defendants, Abdullah & Daud—*Khory & Brydges.*

C. A.

COX, C. J.
and
LAW, J.

1894.

SALWATH HANEEM BINTE ALLIE EFFENDI.
v.
HADJEE ABDULLAH BIN HADJEE MOHAMED CASSIM,
INCHE DAUD BIN HADJEE MOHAMED CASSIM
AND HAIJEE ARSHAD.

YEOH SIEW BEE NEO AND LIM CHEE BOO (HER HUSBAND.)

v.

LEE TENG SEE, LEE TENG THYE, LEE TENG SEANG, LEE HAI THYE AND LEE TOON HUAH.

[PENANG.]

Voluntary Settlement. Consideration. Assignment of Freehold burdened with quit-rent—Subsequent purchaser for value—27 Eliz. c. 4.

L. P. Y. being the owner of a freehold property which under the original Government Grant was subject to a payment to the Crown of a

small annual quit-rent conveyed the same without consideration to the
Defendants in fee in trust for his grandchildren   Subsequently L. P. Y.
being in need of money conveyed the same property to the Plaintiff Y.S.B.N.
in fee for value.   The Plaintiffs thereafter commenced this action praying
for a Declaration that the said Trust Deed was void against the Plaintiff
Y.S.B.N. as a subsequent purchaser for value.

Held that the fact that the Defendants took the property subject to the
burden for the quit-rent did not constitute any consideration for the conveyance to them so as to make it other than a voluntary conveyance.   And that
the conveyance was therefore void against the Plaintiffs under 27 Eliz. c. 4.

Price v. Jenkins, (L. R. 5 Ch. D. 619) distinguished.

GATTY, J.
1894.
Jan. 3.
June 6 & 26.
July 30.

IN addition to the facts stated in the judgment it is only necessary
to add that the original Government Grants (Deeds Poll) were
from The East India Company to the several grantees therein named
" their heirs and assigns for ever " of the lands in question subject
to an annual quit-rent of one copong (10 cents) per orlong per annum.
The Plaintiff Yeoh Siew Bee Neo paid $4.000 as the price of the
lands.

The point having been argued on the 3rd of January and judgment reserved, it was further argued at the request of the Court on
the 6th and 26th of June.

Van Someren for the Plaintiff contended that the Trust Deed was
void under the 27th Eliz. c. 4 and that the fact of the property being burdened with the payment of a quit-rent did not of itself constitute valuable consideration for the Deed.   [*GATTY J.* referred to *Price v. Jenkins
v. sup.*]   That was a case of leasehold and did not apply, as here the
property is freehold.   The Court would not extend the principle of
Price v. Jenkins especially as it had been commented on unfavourably
in the following cases.   *Ex parte Hilman*, (L. R. 10 Ch. D. 622.)   *In
re Ridler*, (L. R. 22 Ch. D. 74.)   *In re Marsh*, (L. R. 24 Ch. D. 11.)
*Shurmur v. Sedgwick, (*Ibid 597.)   *In re Lulham*, (53 L. J. Ch. 928.)
Green v. Paterson, (L. R. 32 Ch. D. 95.)   *Harris v. Tubb*, (L. R. 42
Ch. D. 79.) and the Court of Appeal in Ireland had refused to follow it.
Lee v. Mathews, (L R. 6 Ir. App. 530.)   *May* on Voluntary Conveyances
(2nd Ed.) p. 258.

Secondly.   The Defendants were not personally liable, as the
original Government Grants were Deeds Poll and the words imposing
the quit-rent " subject to an annual quit-rent of one copong per
orlong per annum " did not amount to a covenant on the part of the
grantee to pay the quit-rent.   *Wolveridge v. Steward* (1 Cr. and

Mees. 644). The case of *East India Coy. v. Lonr* (1 Kyshe 78.) was not a considered judgment and was inconsistent with the case last cited.

Thirdly. The remedy by the Crown for non-payment of quit-rent was only by distress. Land Regulation 1 of 1831 sec. 8 cl. 3, Indian Act XVI of 1839 sec. 10 cl. 5, and Ord. IV of 1886 secs. 5, 6 and 7.

Gawthorne for the Defendants submitted that the case of *Price v. Jenkins* applied and governed this case.

GATTY, J.

1894.

YEOH SIEW BL
NEO AND
LIM CHEE BOO
HER HUSBAND.

v.

LEE TENG SRR.
LEE TENG
THYE, LEE
TENG SEANG,
LEE HAI THYE,
AND LEE
TOON HUAM.

C. A. V.

LAW, J. read the following written judgment which had been prepared by *GATTY, J.*

In this case the Plaintiff claims a declaration that the conveyance named in the writ made by one Lee Phee Yeow should be declared void on the ground that it was a voluntary conveyance given for no consideration.

The Defendants in their statements of Defence admit the allegation in the Plaintiff's statement of Claim and thereby if this case is to be decided on pleadings alone admit that the deed in question was a voluntary conveyance and made without valuable consideration given therefor. The Defendants however being Trustees, I have felt bound to consider not only their plea but the merits of the case and to decide the important question which the admitted facts of the case involve whether or no there can be in this Colony such a thing as a voluntary conveyance of lands burdened with the payment of a quit-rent to the Crown, having regard to the principle laid down in the case of *Price v. Jenkins* (L. R. 5 Ch: D. 619) where it was held that there could be no such thing as a voluntary conveyance of leaseholds inasmuch as the lessee was burdened with an implied covenant to pay the rent constituting some valuable consideration sufficient to support the Deed and prevent its being voluntary.

It is not without considerable hesitation that I have come to the conclusion that the decision in *Price v. Jenkins* does not govern this case so as to entitle the Defendants to the judgment of the Court in their favour.

The Deeds Poll from the East India Company or the Crown are not in the strict sense of the term leases for they are wanting in the first element of a lease which is a nveyance of lands or tenements

GATTY, J. but always for a less term than the party conveying himself has in
1894. the premises. They are therefore assignments and not leases and I
YEOH SIEW BEE further observe that they are not deeds executed by the grantee as
NEO AND
LIM CHER BOO well as the grantor.
HER HUSBAND.
v.
LEE TENG SEE,   It appears to me to be unnecessary for the purposes of this case,
LEE TENG
THYE, LEE to decide whether or not a personal liability attaches to the grantee
TENG SEANG,
LEE HAI THYE, in which the grantor could bring an action of debt or covenant against
AND LEE
TOON HUAH. the assignee of the grantee of the lands conveyed in addition to the
grantor's statutory remedy by distress.

Having regard to the decisions of Irish Judges on the subject,
and the doubts which have been expressed by English Judges upon
the principle laid down in the case of *Price v. Jenkins* and also to
the insignificant amount of the quit-rent reserved in comparison to
the value of the land, I have come to the conclusion that I should be
straining the law if I were to hold that the incidence of the small
charge on the land constituted valuable consideration passing from
the grantees to the grantor so as to uphold this conveyance which,
in other respects, is undoubtedly voluntary.

My judgment therefore must be for the Plaintiff in the terms
of the indorsement upon the Writ of Summons. I do not however
consider this to be a case in which the Defendants, who are trustees,
should be mulcted in costs, and as to these therefore I make no
order.

Solicitor for the Plaintiff.—*R. G. Van Someren.*
Solicitor for the Defendants.—*T. Gawthorne.*

AHVENA RAVENA MANA ABOOMOOGUM CHITTY.

v.

LIM AH HANG, AH GEE AND CHOP LEE WATT.

[SINGAPORE.]

Promissory Note.   Immoral Consideration.

Where money was lent on a promissory note for the purposes of working a brothel.

Held that it could not be recovered.

THE facts of the case appear fully in the judgment.

COX, C. J.
1894.
May 11.

Koek for Plaintiff cited :—

Ordinance XIV of 1888.

Quarrier v. Colston (1 Phil. 147.)

King v. Kemp (8 L. T. N. S. 255.)

D'Almeida v. D'Menzies (4 Kyshe 126.)

Joaquim for Defendants cited :—

Bowry v. Bennet (1 Camp. 348.)

Cannan v. Bryce (3 B. & Ald. 179.)

McKinnell v. Robinson (3 M. & W. 434.)

Girardy v. Robinson (1 Esp. 13.)

Pearce v. Brooks (L. R. 1 Exch. 213.)

Smith v. White (L. R. 1 Eq. 626.)

Waugh v. Morris (L. R. 8 Q. B. 202.)

Byles on Bills of Exchange p. 156.

COX, C. J.

This is an action brought by the Plaintiff against the Defendants to recover a sum of $630 balance due on a Promissory Note. One of the Defendants Ah Gee is keeper of a brothel in Fraser Street under the chop "Lee Watt" and that chop is also sued. The Defendants do not deny making the Promissory Note, but allege that they only received $600 on the note and not $690 the consideration named therein, the $90 representing interest which was added to the principal. The defence really is that the amount was received by the Defendant Ah Gee and was to the knowledge of the Plaintiff borrowed for the purpose of buying jewellery and clothing for the inmates of her brothel. For the Defendants it was contended that the object of the contract being immoral no action can lie. The Plaintiff does not admit that he knew that the money was borrowed for that purpose, but both the Defendants have sworn that the money was borrowed for the purpose of keeping the brothel going, that the Plaintiff was in the habit of going to the brothel every day to receive the instalments payable under the Promissory Note, namely, $6 a day and this sum of $6 was from the proceeds of the earnings of the inmates of the brothel the night previous. and they gave evidence of similar transactions which the Plaintiff had with other establishments of the same kind in the same street. The Plaintiff swore that he was

COX, C. J.

1894.

ANVERA RAVE-
NA MANA
ARCOMOOGUM
CHITTY.

v.

LIM AH HANG
AH GEE AND
CHOP LEE
WATT.

not aware that the money borrowed was for the purpose of keeping the brothel, but that it was represented to him by the Defendants that it was required for the business of the first Defendant who also carried on the business of a rickisha owner. Upon these facts I am satisfied that the evidence given by the Defendants should be accepted. I find it proved that when the Plaintiff lent the money he knew it was required for the purpose of working the brothel. Upon these facts I hold the maxim *ex turpi causa non oritur actio* applies and the Plaintiff cannot recover. In *Cannan v. Bryce* (*v. sup.*) the principle was clearly laid down that the repayment of money lent for the express purpose of accomplishing an illegal object cannot be enforced. Mr. Koek contended that in this Colony the trade was not illegal and called my attention to the Women and Girls' Protection Ordinance No. XIV of 1888 which provides for the Registration of Brothels, but I cannot accept that argument and I hold as I have already said that when the maxim *ex turpi causa non oritur actio* applies, no action lies. This is clearly laid down in *Pearce v. Brooks* (*v. sup.*) which was the case of a coachbuilder who sued a prostitute for the hire of a brougham. Upon the facts there held, Pollock C. B. says " Nor can any distinction be made between an " illegal and an immoral purpose ; the rule which is applicable to the " matter is *ex turpi causa non oritur actio* ; and whether it is an " immoral or an illegal purpose in which the Plaintiff has parti- " cipated, it comes equally within the terms of the maxim and the " effect is the same ; no cause of action can arise out of the one or the " other." This appears clear and on the authorities of *Cannan v. Bryce* and *Pearce v. Brooks* I hold that this action cannot lie and must be dismissed with costs.

Judgment for Defendants.

Solicitor for Plaintiff—*E. R. Koek.*
Solicitors for Defendants—*Joaquim Brothers.*

MAGISTRATES APPEALS.
REG. ON THE PROSECUTION OF TEO BUN CHUN, APPELLANT.
v.

TEO AH SOON AND NG HA ENG. RESPONDENTS.
[SINGAPORE.]

Criminal Law—Appeal against acquittal on question of fact. The

Appeals Ordinance 1879 (XII of 1879)—Prosecutor summarily fined under Section 103 of Indian Act. XIII of 1856 for frivolous prosecution.

Where a Magistrate has upon a mere question of fact acquitted a Defendant the Supreme Court will not interfere.

The grounds for fining a prosecutor under Section 103 of Indian Act. XIII of 1856 discussed.

COX, C. J.
1884.
Oct. 15.

TEO AH SOON and NG HA ENG were charged before J. O. Anthonisz, Esq., on October 15th, with the theft of certain articles of clothing from the house of Teo Bun Chun. The prosecutor stated that he was at work in a field near his house when he saw the prisoners come out of the house. He went and examined his box and found some of his property missing. He followed the two men and gave them into custody. He alleged that some of the missing property was found on the men The Magistrate dismissed the charge against the accused, and imposed a fine of $10 on the prosecutor, under sec. 103, Indian Act XIII of 1856, for instituting a frivolous prosecution.

L. P. Van Cuylenburg for the Appellant. The Magistrate had no jurisdiction to deal with the case summarily as the charge was one of theft from a dwelling house. Secondly the decision was against the weight of evidence. Besides that of the prosecutor there was the evidence of the police constable. Thirdly he evidence *did* show sufficient ground for making a charge and the Magistrate should not have imposed the fine of $10. It lay in his discretion to inflict a fine for a frivolous prosecution, but in this case there were no sufficient grounds for exercising that discretion.

COX, C. J.

This is an appeal from a decision of a Magistrate in Singapore, by which he dismissed a charge of theft of the property of Teo Bun Chun against Teo Ah Soon and Ng Ha Eng. The Magistrate after hearing the evidence dismissed the charge and further ruled that there were no sufficient grounds for making that charge. Under section 103 of Indian Act XIII of 1856 he ordered the prosecutor to pay $10 damages to the two defendants for their loss of time and expenses in going to Court. I am asked to reverse these two decisions, to say that the men should be convicted of the charge on the evidence, and to set aside the order of the Magistrate with regard to the $10 imposed. It is not clear that this Court may on appeal convict men who have been

COX, C. J.

1894.

REG. ON THE
PROSECUTION
OF
TEO BUN CHUN,
APPELLANT.
v.
TEO AH SOON
AND
NG BA ENG,
RESPONDENTS.

acquitted by the Magistrate on a pure question of fact. No doubt when a Magistrate gives a wrong decision on a point of law the Court can revise it, and quash it and send the case back for further prosecution. But I am not satisfied that under the Appeals Ordinance this Court has power, when an accused has been tried and acquitted on a clear issue of fact, to reverse the decision and convict him. Even if I considered the Court had that power, in this case I should not exercise it. The Magistrate heard the evidence and was satisfied that the charge was not made out. I therefore decline to convict these men. With regard to the second part of the decision, that stands upon different ground. The Magistrate has not only declined to convict the men, but has fined the prosecutor by way of awarding damages to the accused, because he thought there were not sufficient grounds for the charge. I am unable to agree with the Magistrate. In reality there were two witnesses who gave evidence in support of the charge, the plaintiff himself who says he saw two men come out of his house. He chased them and the men were arrested. That was supported by the evidence of the police-constable. The Magistrate may have had some reason to hold that the evidence was not strong enough to support a conviction, entailing imprisonment perhaps for several months. But I cannot hold that there was such absence of proof in support of the charge that the complainant should be punished for having set the law in motion. I therefore set aside the order of the Magistrate fining the Appellant $10.

Solicitor for the Appellants.—*L. P. Van Cuylenburg.*

REG. ON THE PROSECUTION OF E. H. BELL, RESPONDENT.

v.

JOHN BURNETT PAIGE, APPELLANT.

[SINGAPORE.]

Criminal Law—Arms Exportation Ordinance 1887 (XVIII of 1887).

The evidence required to convict a person of exporting articles contrary to the provisions of the Arms Exportation Ordinance 1887 (XVIII of 1887) discussed.

JOHN BURNETT PAIGE was convicted on October 22nd, 1894, COLLYER, J.
before W. Egerton and J. O. Anthonisz, Esqrs., that he did in
partnership with certain others on or about April 16th, export from
Singapore to Bali, a part of Netherlands India, a quantity of arms,
to wit, rifles, contrary to the provisions of section 4 of the Arms
Exportation Ordinance 1887 (XVIII of 1887).   He was fined $1,000.
Against this decision he appealed, the grounds of appeal being (1)
that there was no evidence to support a conviction, and (2) that the
Magistrates were wrong in law in holding that a partner is criminally liable for the acts of his co-partners.

W. Nanson for the Appellant.

A. L. Donaldson for the Respondent and the Netherlands India
authorities.

The evidence having been read, *Nanson* contended that there was
no evidence to show that the arms had been exported from Singapore,
and, even if there was, that there was no evidence that the Appellant
had anything to do with the arms.   It was not shown that he had
bought the arms, nor that he had anything to do with getting them
on board.   He further urged that the legal presumption was against
the captain and not against his client, whilst he contended that in law
the Appellant was not criminally liable for the acts of his co-partners.
True, there were suspicious circumstances in the case.   This man was
found with arms at Bali, but that he explained by saying that while
on a voyage to New Guinea they were driven ashore by misfortune at
Bali, and their whole conduct was consistent with that explanation.
Nothing would have been easier than for them to have hidden the
arms in the sand, whilst the Dutch officials also treated them as
shipwrecked mariners.   The Appellant said he had no idea that
there were arms on board until a short time before they reached Bali,
that the arms were improperly purchased, and that Danielsen, the
captain of the ship, was never instructed to buy arms.

Donaldson submitted that the nominal pearling agreement was
a bogus one, and that the $3,000 subscribed amongst the parties
to the agreement was an enormous sum for a pearling expedition.   Of
this $900 was spent on the boat and $50 for the hire of a diving
apparatus, whilst a further sum was to be spent on provisions.   In-
stead of that they found it admitted that a considerable sum was spent
in arms and ammunition, and that when the boat reached Bali there

COLLYER, J. were a number of cases of arms and ammunition on board. There
1894. was evidence also that arms were purchased in Singapore, and that
Reg. on the the arms on board were of a peculiar description, precisely similar to
Prosecution
of some which had been sold to a man named Niel. They could not give
E. H. Bell,
Respondent direct evidence of what was in a man's mind; his motives could only
v. be inferred by his precedent or subsequent acts, and the question was
John Burnett
Paige, whether this was a *bona fide* pearling expedition or merely an
Appellant. arms expedition under cover of a pearling expedition. The Defendant's
conduct was such as to show that he was a party to the arms expedition, and that he must have known there were arms on board; and it
was actually in evidence that he assisted in the loading of the ponies
which carried a portion of the arms into the interior. That the
pearling expedition was not *bona fide* was shown from the Defendant's
story. It was impossible to believe that they intended to proceed to
New Guinea, a distance of 1,000 miles, and there dive for pearls,
after they had lost both their anchors off Tanah Tjina.

Nanson replied.

COLLYER, J.

I had at first some doubt whether there was sufficient evidence to
go before a jury. It is true there is not much of it, but I have come
to the conclusion that it is one of those cases I would leave to a jury;
and when once it has got before a jury there is very little doubt that
a conviction would ensue. It is perfectly true that what the men did in
Bali had not much to do with it. If they really had been cheated by
Danielsen and, finding themselves unexpectedly on the coast of Bali
with a cargo of arms, had then decided to make best of a difficult
position, there would have been nothing contrary to the law of this
Colony in their getting rid of these arms by selling them. The
question is whether there has been anything which can be considered
as evidence of Paige's being a party to the exportation of these arms
from Singapore. It is pretty clear what view the Magistrates took,
and I think probably they were right. They said here is a case of
arms being exported by a small boat from Singapore and taken to
Bali, there being only a small number of persons on board, who
declared they were going to New Guinea in ballast. The circumstances
with regard to that are such as to induce us to believe that the
pearling expedition was a sham one, and that those who started on
that expedition were simply engaged in exporting arms for sale. The

persons who were parties in the expedition were Danielsen for one and Paige for another. There was ample reason to think—unless they thought Paige was innocent or extremely simple—that he must have known that this agreement was a sham agreement, and that the real object of the expedition was something entirely different. Then in that case, this being a sham expedition for the purpose of exporting arms, the evidence against Paige was his presence from first to last, and his being the owner of the vessel. The actual paragraphs in the depositions which pointed to Paige being concerned in this matter were very small, but I think the evidence quite sufficient to show that he was one of the several persons who were shamming to gô on a pearling expedition, but who really were engaged in exporting arms. I think there can be no doubt that Paige was concerned in the expedition. Then there is the impression made by the man's own evidence. I am not inclined to upset the verdict of the Magistrates on the ground that the verdict was against the weight of evidence, and I certainly shall not do so in this case, because it seems to me probable that they were right. If anything, the statement by Paige added to the evidence against him. I do not know that any one can really believe that the man, who is an engineer and a practical man, a man of discretion, would have joined an expedition of that sort under that agreement if it had been a *bona fide* agreement. For these reasons I am not inclined to interfere with the judgment in the Court below.

Marginal note: COLLYER, J. 1894. Reg. on the Prosecution of E. H. Bell, Respondent. *v.* John Burnett Paige, Appellant.

Conviction affirmed.

Donaldson applied for costs. *Nanson* objected. This was an appeal against the Crown.

No costs were allowed.

Solicitors for the Appellant.—*Rodyk & Davidson.*
Solicitors for the Respondent.—*Donaldson & Burkinshaw.*

NAIVANA MAYANA MEYAPPAH CHITTY BY HIS ATTORNEY MOOTAYAH CHITTY.

v.

MOHOMET SHAIK AND MAHOMET EBRAM KHAN.

[PENANG.]

Mortgage—Right to sue on covenant after sale of property.

After a mortgagee has exercised his power of sale he can still sue on his covenant for the balance of principal and interest due.

GATTY, J.
1894
June 29.

THIS was an action brought to recover the residue of principal and interest due on a mortgage made some ten years before the commencement of the suit. The property had been sold and the mortgage deed lost.

Shearwood for the defendants, contended that (apart from the denial of the indebtedness on facts) if the property had been foreclosed and parted with, this action could not be brought. The principles governing a foreclosure suit in this particular equally apply to a sale. When a mortgagee had foreclosed, he could not sue on his covenant without reopening the foreclosure as on payment in full he was bound to reconvey the property. When he had parted with it, he could not do this and thereby was debarred from suing, an injunction lying to prevent him. *Palmer v. Hendrie* (27 Beav. 349, 28 Beav. 341) where the mortgagee concurred with the transferee of the equity of redemption in selling the estate and allowed the transferee to receive the purchase money. Also *Lockhart v. Hardy* (9 Beav. 349).

There did not appear to be any precise precedent for adopting this doctrine in the case of a sale, but the principles were the same. *Rudge v. Richens* (L. R. 8 C. P. 358) apparently to the contrary was decided on a point of pleading under the practice before the Judicature Acts as to striking out a bad plea and hence is not applicable. The mortgagee covenants to reconvey on repayment and when the property is sold he cannot do so.

Adams (*E. Farrer-Baynes* with him) *contra*. A power of sale is inserted in almost every mortgage, and such powers would be useless if the mortgagee had no further remedy for the rest of his money. A distinction is to be drawn between a foreclosure which is against the consent of the mortgagor and a sale which is by his express consent. This distinction is well illustrated in *Kinnaird v. Trollope* (L. R. 39 Ch. D. 636) where Stirling J. says on page 465 :—In *Palmer v. Hendrie*, it was held " that the mortgagor on paying off the mortgage debt was entitled to have the property restored to him unaffected by any acts of the mortgagee unauthorized by the mortgagor. The necessary authority might be derived either as in the case of *Rudge v. Richens* (L. R. 8. C. P. 358) from the powers conferred by the mortgage deed or from the direct concurrence of the mortgagor or possibly otherwise ; but it was held in *Palmer v. Hendrie* that the mere concurrence of the assignee of the equity of redemption in acts which were not within the powers conferred by the mortgage was insufficient."

Mr. Prideaux in his *Precedents* after quoting the doctrine laid down in *Palmer v. Hendrie* continues. " but this of course does not apply to a sale by a mortgagee who has not foreclosed under his power of sale " (1 Prid: Prec. 14 Ed: 492).

GATTY. J.

On the authority of *Kinnaird v. Trollope* I decide in favour of the mortgagee, and the action is properly brought. When there is a power of sale in a mortgage deed either statutory or expressly inserted, it is there with the consent of the mortgagor, who, by allowing a sale waives his right to have the property restored on repayment.

Judgment for plaintiff with costs.

Solicitors for the plaintiff. —*Hogan & Adams.*

Solicitor for the defendants.—*J. A. Shearwood.*

REGINA

v.

VALI MUTU SIVAM.

PENANG.

Extradition.—Queen's Order in Council. 19th August 1889—Minister of State.

The Secretary to Government, Perak, is not a " Minister of State " within section 13. clause 2 of the Order in Council. dated the 19th August, 1889. Hence his seal is no authentication of a judicial document.

THIS was an application for a writ of *Habeas Corpus* to obtain the release of one Vali Mutu Sivam who had been committed to prison by Mr. Haughton, Acting Chief Magistrate of Penang, under clause 16 of the Queen's Order in Council dated the 19th August 1889, with the view to extradite him to Perak for an offence committed there.

The facts were as follows :

Vali Mutu Sivam was overseer of certain coolies employed in Public Works by the Perak Government in 1891. It was alleged that on certain occasions he employed them in private work for himself and put them down in the pay sheet as having worked for Govern-

GATTY, J.

1894.

NAIVANA MATANA ME-YAPPA CHITTY BY HIS ATTORNEY MOO-TAYAH CHITTY.

v.

MAHOMET SHAIK AND MA-HOMET EBRAM KNAN.

LAW, J.

1894.

Aug. 3.

LAW, J.

1894.

REGINA
v.
VALI MUTU
SIVAM

ment on those days. Some coolies admitted this to Mr. Bird when holding an inquiry at Parit Buntar. A warrant was issued by a Perak Magistrate in 1891, but the man was not found till last June, when Mr. Haughton granted a provisional warrant on the information of Detective Inspector Fiddes, stating the fact that he had received a telegram from Perak in 1891 and other matters of which he had been informed. On the requisition for extradition arriving from Perak, the Governor issued his order directing the Magistrate to inquire into the charge. A warrant was then granted on the evidence of the Perak documents, and the accused brought before Mr. Haughton, Mr. Bird and others appearing as witnesses and he was committed to prison in the usual course to wait the Governor's order for his rendition.

J. Shearwood on behalf of the prisoner obtained a rule *nisi* to show cause why a writ of *Habeas Corpus* should not be granted.

The grounds for the application were :

1. There was no evidence before the Magistrate that the alleged act was a crime by the law of Perak.

2. The offence of cheating by falsification of documents of which the prisoner was accused is not one of the crimes in the Schedule to Order of Council of 1889.

3. The prisoner proved before the Magistrate that he was a British subject born in Ceylon ; the word " shall " appearing in 37 and 38 Vict. c. 38 gives exclusive jurisdiction to the Colony and prevents rendition elsewhere.

4. There was no evidence to justify the granting of the warrant as the judicial documents on which it was granted were not authenticated.

The case was argued on the return of the rule *nisi* before Mr. Justice Law when the Solicitor-General (*D. Logan*) showed cause.

The case is reported only with regard to the question raised by the fourth point. The Solicitor-General's arguments fully appear in the judgment.

Shearwood contra. The Order in Council of 1889 lays down that the Magistrate shall inquire into the truth of the charge and issue a warrant at his discretion on the evidence produced. Hence there must be some evidence (*Reg. v. Weil* I. R. 9 Q. B. D. 705. *Sirdar Khan's case* II Kyshe 57). Here there is none. The Perak information and

LAW. J.
1894.
REGINA
v.
VALI MUTU
SIVAN.

warrant were signed by a Magistrate whose position and signature were authenticated by the signature and official seal of the Acting Secretary to Government, and sec. 13 of the order provides that these must be authenticated by the oath of a witness or the seal of a Minister of State. It was decided in *Reg. v. Wong Ah Kam* (IV Kyshe 150) that the British Resident of Perak was not a Minister of State and his official seal was no authentication of a document, and in *Sirdar Khan's* case that he could not make a requisition for rendition under the order of 1879. These decisions were when the old orders were in force. The new order rectified sec. 1 by inserting the words in sec. 3 " or in the case of any of the Protected States, &c." and thus enabled the Resident and Secretary to Government to make a requisition, but it left sec. 8 untouched, the verbiage of sec. 13 of the new order being similar to sec. 8 of the old one. Hence the seal of the Resident is no authentication. The seal of the Secretary to Government stands on a similar footing. The insertion in sec. 3 shows they were designed to be considered in the same light.

Also the term " State " means a Sovereign and not a dependent or Semi-Sovereign State.

LAW, J.

The most important question raised in this case was I think the question of whether the words Minister of State in sec. 13 sub-section 2 of the extradition Order in Council are to be held to include the Secretary to Government in Perak. No authorities were quoted to me to show sufficiently what exactly " Minister of State " must be held to mean, and I know of none. I must try therefore though with much diffidence to show what it seems to me the ordinary meaning of these words must be taken to be. It appears to me that the words " Minister of State " refer to a Minister or Officer of Government who theorically at any rate is only subordinate to the Sovereign or other Chief or Supreme ruling authority. By the consent of the parties the Perak Hand-Book was put in to assist me in forming some opinion as to the status of the Secretary to Government in Perak and from the Hand-Book I gather, and indeed I should suppose it is notorious, that the Secretary to Government in Perak is subordinate to and under the order of the British Resident, who himself again is under the orders of the Governor of the Straits Settlements. I may then at once say, that it does not seem to me the words Minister of

State, would ordinarily include the Secretary to Government in Perak.

Mr. *Logan* however argued as I understand, that the difference of the wording which has been introduced into clause 3 of the extradition Order in Council 1889, from that which existed in prior Orders in Council, this amendment of wording being effected after the ruling of Mr. Justice Wood in the case of *Reg. v. Wong Ah Kam* (IV Kyshe p. 150) to the effect that the words Minister of State do not include the British Resident of Perak, showed an intention to get rid of all difficulties that might arise, from the British Resident or the Secretary to Government not being held to be Ministers of State, and that therefore in section 13 (2) above referred to, the words Minister of State must be held to include the British Residents and the Secretaries to Government in the Protected States; but if this view was correct, the simplest plan would I should think have been to enact that the words Minister of State should be held to include the British Residents and the Secretaries to Government in Protected States. Again clause 3 deals with requisitions for the surrender of fugitive offenders and clause 13 (2) with authentication of documents—an entirely different thing. In the old Order in Council of 1879 power was given as it is in the order of 1889 to Consuls and vice Consuls as well as to Ministers of State to make requisitions for the surrender of fugitive offenders, though Consuls and vice Consuls are not I think Ministers of State, see *In Re Piper* (IV Kyshe p. 221). I cannot then see that conferring on British Residents and Secretaries to Government in the Protected States, power as to requisitions for the surrender of fugitive offenders which were previously enjoyed by some persons who were not Ministers of State, is evidence of an intention to confer on British Residents and Secretaries to Government the same powers as are clearly enjoyed by Ministers of State under the Order in Council in respect of authentication of documents.

In my opinion the warrant and depositions from Perak have not been properly authenticated and as it is not contended that the Magistrate's warrant of apprehension was issued on any other evidence I think there was no evidence on which the Magistrate was justified in issuing a warrant for Sivam's arrest and that the writ asked for must issue.

Rule absolute.   Prisoner discharged from custody.

Solicitor for the Applicant.—*J. A. Shearwood.*

SHEENA SAIBOO

v.

PANA SILTEE MOHAMED AND OTHERS.

PENANG.

Account stated—Indian Limitation Act XIV of 1859 Sec. 1 (9).

An account stated but not signed by the person sued does not constitute an implied contract so as to allow a period of six years for suit from the time of the stating of the account.

A PROMISSORY Note for the amount claimed in a settled account had been given by persons whom the plaintiff alleged to be the defendants' partners to one M. Zein in 1888 and was by him assigned to the plaintiff.

On the note being tendered in evidence it was found to be insufficiently stamped and impounded and being a negotiable instrument could not be given in evidence even on tender of the penalty.

Leave was then given to amend the writ on payment of costs so as to allow the plaintiff to sue as equitable assignee of an account stated.

Farrer Baynes for the defendant. The claim is barred. (*H. D. Tripp v. Kubeer Mundul* 9 W. R. 209) and other cases cited in Thomson's Limitation of Civil Suits (2nd Ed. pp. 140-2).

In *Jones v. Ryder* (4 M. & W. 32). it was held that a promissory note improperly stamped was not admissible as a memorandum to take the case out of the Statute of Limitations. There the action was on an account stated.

Shearwood contra. In *Umedchand Hukamchand v. Sha Bulakidas Lalchand* (5 Bom. H. C. 16), also Thomson's Limitation of Civil Suits (p. 138) it was decided that an account stated is founded on a contract implied by law and falls under clause 16 of Indian Act XIV of 1859. (section 1) thus giving six years from the time of settling the account.

The fact of its being signed is not relied upon in that case as a ground for the decision.

LAW, J.

In the case last cited the account stated was signed; *see Doyle v. Allum Biswas* (4 W. R., S. C. 1), Thomson's Limitation of Civil Suits (p. 140) where it was decided that the verbal stating of an account does not create a fresh liability. This is strengthened by *Jones v. Ryder.* I rule the claim is barred.

Solicitors for the Plaintiff.—*J. A. Shearwood.*

Solicitors for the Defendants.—*Hogan & Adams.*

LAW, J.
1894
Aug. 7, 8, 9, 15,
16, 21, 22, 23, 25,
27, and 28 and
Sept. 10.

THE OWNERS OF THE S.S. "KWANG TUNG"

v.

THE OWNERS OF THE S.S. "NGAPOOTA."

[PENANG.]

*Collision—Articles 15 and 18—Evidence—Admissions—The Evidence
Ordinance 1893 Sections 145 and 157.*

The depositions of witnesses taken at a Marine Court of Enquiry if
properly proved may be used to contradict the testimony of the same persons
when called to give evidence in an action for damages arising from collision. Statements made by a captain of a ship to a reporter of a newspaper
are admissible as admissions against the owners of the ship. When once a
ship is within a rule requiring her to take or keep a definite course she cannot
whilst the risk continues come within the operation of any other rule requiring her to adopt a different manoeuvre.

A person navigating a ship is entitled to a very short time within which
to exercise his judgment whether to reverse or not under Article 19 of the
Regulations for Preventing Collisions at Sea.

THIS was a claim and counter-claim for damages, each vessel
alleging the other to be solely to blame for a collision which
occurred on the 24th April last, some 13 miles N. W. of Tanjong
Hantu in the Straits of Malacca. The following is a narrative of the
collision.

The British steamer *Kwang Tung*, official No. 89,142 of the port
of Penang, Henry Cobb, master, left Penang with 137 passengers and
a crew of 36 for Teluk Anson on the 23rd April, about 5 p.m. At
about 12.30 a.m. the Captain being on deck, a white light was sighted
ahead. On his looking through binoculars it was discovered to be a
steamer shewing her three lights. The *Kwang Tung's* helm was then
ported about a point, and shortly after the green light was shut in
and the red and white lights only were showing on the port bow.
The ships continued thus until they were a little less than ½ a mile off,
when the s.s. *Ngapoota* again showed her three lights. The *Kwang
Tung's* helm was then put hard-a-port. Almost immediately the
Ngapoota's red light was shut in, and directly this happened the
Kwang Tung's engines were stopped and put full speed astern and
the whistle was blown. Less than half a minute afterwards
the *Kwang Tung* struck the *Ngapoota* at right angles about
amidships on the starboard side. The *Ngapoota* sank almost immediately. The *Kwang Tung* burned blue lights and rockets and lowered three boats, and on being found to be making water badly was
headed for the shore. One of the boats followed her and the others
remained at the sunken ship. The *Kwang Tung* sunk at about
2.15 a.m. in 3 fathoms of water. The passengers and crew remained

LAW, J.
1894.

THE OWNERS OF
THE S.S.
"KWANG TUNG"
v.
THE OWNERS OF
THE S.S.
"NGAPOOTA."

on top of the awning in the rigging till the morning, when they taken off by tongkang No. 130, 32 having left during the night in the remaining boat. Seven of the passengers and one of the crew were subsequently discovered to be missing.

The British steamer *Ngapoota*, official No. 68,511 of the port of London, G. H. A. Witt, master, carrying a crew of 30 and 85 passengers, making a total of 115 souls on board, left Teluk Anson on the 23rd April. at 5.30 p.m.. for Penang, calling at Pangkor on her way. After leaving Pangkor she steered her course for Penang. After clearing Pulau Hantu and getting into open water, at 11.50 p.m., the Captain left the serang in charge of the deck, telling him to steer N.N.W. and went into his cabin which is on the bridge. At about 12.30 a.m. the gunner John Brasset, who had relieved the deck at midnight, states that he saw a white light and then a green light ahead; soon afterwards seeing the green light very close on his starboard bow. he called the Captain. The Captain came out and, seeing a green light close on the starboard bow. ordered the helm hard-a-starboard, and says he blew the steam whistle twice. Immediately afterwards she was struck on the starboad side amidships, foundering within five minutes. Her port boat being the only one uninjured was lowered and 48 persons got into her. The Captain and a few others kept themselves afloat on the wreckage, and four men were taken off the mast in the morning. Forty-five passengers and crew being reported as missing after full enquiries had been made.

S. R. Groom and *R. A. P. Hogan* appeared for the s.s. *Kwang, Tung*.

F. J. C. Ross. R. G. Van Someren and *G. H. Maylor* for the s.s. *Ngapoota*.

During the cross examination of Captain Cobb, the master of the *Kwang Tung. Ross* tendered as evidence a previous statement made by the witness in the Marine Court of Enquiry and inconsistent with the statement now made. The previous statement was tendered under the provisions of sec. 145 of the Evidence Act to contradict.

Groom.— The statement made in the Marine Court of Enquiry is not relevant to the issue now before the Court. The parties are not the same. The plaintiffs in the present action were not and could not be represented and could not examine the witness. The test is, could statements on Marine Court of Enquiry be put in under sec. 157 to

LAW, J.
1894.

THE OWNERS OF
THE S.S.
"KWANG TUNG"
v.
THE OWNERS OF
THE S.S.
"NGAPOOTA."

corroborate testimony of witness ?   The finding of the Marine Court of Enquiry not being relevant, the proceedings on which finding is based are not relevant.   He quoted *The Little Lizzie* (L. R. 3 A. and E. 56), *The Henry Coxon* (L. R. 3 P. D. 156) and *Nothard v. Pepper* (17 C. B. N. S. 39.)

Ross,—It is admitted that the finding of the Marine Court of Enquiry is not relevant, but statements made on a former occasion may be put in under sec. 145 to contradict the witness.   Statements taken before Wreck Commissioners in England may be put in to contradict witnesses at a subsequent trial.   He referred to 17 and 18 Vic. c. 104 sec. 448.

Groom,—The duties of a Wreck Commissioner are distinct from those of a Marine Court of Enquiry.   The section referred to is repealed by 39 and 40 Vic. c. 80 s. 45.   There was then a statutory enactment making such evidence admissible.   In any case the original deposition must be put in.   This cannot be done as they have been sent to the Board of Trade.

[*LAW, J.* I think the former statement may be used for the purpose of contradicting the witnesses.   The depositions tendered for that purpose however must be properly proved.]

At the close of the evidence for the plaintiffs, *Groom* put in a statement made by Captain Witt to the Reporter and subsequently to the Editor of the *Pinang Gazette.*

Ross, for the defendants, objected that it could not be put in, and was not evidence as against the defendants.   The statement was not made at the time the facts occurred.

Groom,—The statement is a fact within the meaning of section 3 of the Evidence Ordinance.   He referred to secs. 5, 8, 9, 11 and *The Solway* (L. R. 10 P. D. 187.)   It is an admission or declaration against his own interest.   In *Ridley v. Gyde* (9 Bing. 349) a declaration made a month after the circumstances arose was admitted in evidence.   In any case the statement is admissible on the ground that the master is the agent of the owners.   He referred to *The Midlothian* (15 Jurist 806) and *The Manchester* (1 W. Rob. 63.)

[*LAW, J.* held that the statement was admissible, and the facts stated therein were inconsistent with facts in issue set up by the defendant.]

Ross for the s.s. *Ngapoota* cited the following cases.

The Ceto (L. R. 14 App. Cas: 670.)

The Jesmond (L. R. 4 P. C. 1.)

The Bywell Castle (L. R. 4 P. D. 219.)

The Beryl (L. R. 9 P. D. 4.)

The Lancashire (L. R. (1894) A. C. 1.)

The Voorwarts and *The Khedive* (L. R. 5 App. Cas. 876.)

The *Arratoon Apcar* (L. R. 15 App. Cas. 37.)

The *Fair Penang* (2 S. L. J. 120.)

Groom for the s.s. *Kwang Tung* besides referring to some of the above cases also cited the following ones.

Chong Moh & Co. v. s.s. Camelot (1 S. S. L. R. 119.)

The Emmy Haase (L. R. 9 P. D. 81.)

The Rhondda (L. R. 8 App. Cas. 549.)

LAW, J.
——
1894.
THE OWNERS OF
THE S.S.
"KWANG TUNG"
v.
THE OWNERS OF
THE S.S.
"NGAPOOTA."

C. A. V.

The judgment of the Court was delivered on the 10th of Sept.

LAW, J.

After considering all the evidence in this case I have come to the conclusion that the story told on behalf of the owners of the *Kwang Tung* is, speaking generally, more correct than that told on behalf of the owners of the *Ngapoota*. There are many circumstances which lead me to view much at any rate of the story told on behalf of the owners of the *Ngapoota* with suspicion. To begin with, Captain Witt himself told shortly after the collision a story to Mr. Palmer and Mr. Kennedy which certainly, as far as I can see, hardly gives an account of his share in the transactions immediately preceding the collision connected with the account which he has given us here in this Court; then again other witnesses on behalf of the *Ngapoota* speak to Captain Witt when he came on the bridge just before the collision, talking about the course and looking at the compass, etc., all of which Captain Witt denies; and Awang, one of the witnesses who now mentions these matters in the Marine Court of Enquiry, said when the Captain came on the bridge the other steamer was quite close.

I think that the evidence tends to shew that there was, to say the least of it, no hurry about calling Captain Witt when the lights of the *Kwang Tung* had been seen and that the evidence further tends to shew that he only got on the bridge a very short time indeed before the collision. Even now Captain Witt says he was awakened by loud shouting which, I think, tends to confirm the view that when he

LAW. J.

1894.

THE OWNERS OF
THE S.S.
"KWANG TUNG"
v.
THE OWNERS OF
THE S.S.
"NGAPOOTA."

awoke an anxious moment had already arrived. Whether Brassett attempted to manœuvre the *Ngapoota* before calling Captain Witt I do not know. He says he did not, and the helmsman says that if Brassett had told him to alter his helm he would not have complied. I doubt if this is true, especially as Captain Witt has said Brassett must have manœuvred the ship to avoid any small boat or to meet any sudden and unforeseen emergency; but whatever the facts may be with regard to this point, it seems to me if Brassett did manœuvre the ship in order to pass the *Kwang Tung* he disobeyed Captain Witt's orders, if he did not, then I think Captain Witt ought to have been called long before he was.

In view of the doubt which I cannot help feeling as to whether Captain Witt was on the bridge in time enough to give any order at all before the collision occurred; of the opinion which I have formed to the effect that, if he was in time to give any such orders, he only arrived just before the collision, and any order given must have been given in a hurry and in a moment of excitement and confusion; of the unfavourable opinion I have formed of most of the evidence given on behalf of the owners of the *Ngapoota*; of the expert evidence which it seems to me must be correct, to the effect that if the red light of the *Kwang Tung* was never visible on the *Ngapoota* before the collision, and the defendants were steering as they say, the collision would not have occurred in the manner described, I believe, as I have already intimated, that substantially it is the story told on behalf of the owners of the *Kwang Tung* that is correct and not that told on behalf of the owners of the *Ngapoota*.

Now the story of the *Kwang Tung* is to the effect that the *Ngapoota* was sighted end on at a distance of some three or four miles off, that thereupon Captain Cobb ported one point which it appears was a perfectly correct thing to do according to the Regulations, that when the *Kwang Tung* got within about $1\frac{1}{4}$ miles of the *Ngapoota* the latter's green light was closed in, that on getting within about $\frac{1}{4}$ a mile all three lights of the *Ngapoota* again became visible, that thereupon Captain Cobb put his helm hard-a-port and blew his whistle and shouted to those on board the *Ngapoota* to port their helm, that seeing the *Ngapoota* swinging round and the red light shut in he gave the order to stop and reverse the engines and that the engines were actually going astern but that the *Ngapoota* ran accross the bows of the

LAW, J.
1894.

THE OWNERS OF
THE S.S.
"KWANG TUNG"
v.
THE OWNERS OF
THE S.S.
"NGAPOOTA."

Kwang Tung which was still going ahead some seven knots an hour, and thus the collision occurred. I believe this to be practically correct, except perhaps in the matter of distances etc., account of what actually happened. It is true that expert evidence has been given to shew that if the ships were at the distance from each other when the three lights all became again visible which Captain Cobb mentioned the collision could not have occurred in the manner described, but Captain Cobb only gives an approximate distance, and it seems to me on the evidence that if the ships were somewhat nearer the collision might quite well have occurred as described; and with regard to this matter and a remark made by one of the witnesses to the effect that in the case of the supposed circles of the *Ngapoota* and *Kwang Tung*, which are shewn as touching on plan "J." the *Ngapoota* would have a longer distance to travel to the point of contact than the *Kwang Tung*, it must, I think, be borne in mind that if the *Ngapoota* first shewed three lights and after that the *Kwang Tung* put her helm hard-a-port the *Ngapoota* must have begun to circle before the *Kwang Tung*. I may just remark here that on the whole of the evidence I think Mr. David must have been mistaken thinking that he saw Captain Cobb starboarding his helm.

It seems to me on the evidence that the *Kwang Tung* did what was correct when the *Ngapoota* was first seen, but it was urged that when the three lights of the *Ngapoota* again became visible the *Kwang Tung* had ceased to be under the end on rule No. 15 and was under the crossing rule. I cannot believe this view is correct, especially as I find the following on the subject in Marsden on Collisions at Sea at page 355, third edition :—

"When two ships are approaching each other with risk of collision, the rule of the road applies once and for all to take them clear. A ship is never required by the Regulations, after having sighted another, to alter her course first to starboard and then to port; or, first to keep her course and then to keep out of the way; or vice versa. In the case, for example, of steamships meeting end on, or nearly so, each is required by Art. 15 to alter her course to starboard. If, while under the port-helm, the relative positions and heading of the ships are changed, so that from meeting ships they become crossing ships, the meeting rule (Art. 15.) does not cease to operate, or give place to the crossing rule (Art. 16). The manœuvre of porting"

LAW, J.

1894.

The Owners of
The S.S.
"Kwang Tung"
v.
The Owners of
The S.S.
"Ngapoota."

"must be persisted in until the risk of collision is determined. If port-
"ing will not take the ships clear, Art. 18 or Art. 23 may apply, and
"the engines may be stopped, or any other step taken which is neces-
"sary to avert collision ; but the ships cannot afterwards, and whilst
"the risk continues, become crossing ships. If once a ship is within
"the meeting rule, or any other rule requiring her to take or keep a
"definite course, or requiring her to keep out of the way, she
"cannot, whilst the risk continues, come within the operation of the
"crossing rule, or any other rule requiring her to adopt a different
"manœuvre. The object of the rule of the road and of the Re-
"gulations would be entirely frustrated if it were possible for a
"ship to be thrown from one rule to another, if, whilst in the act of
"obeying one article, she were suddenly to come within the operation
"of another rule, requiring her perhaps to take an exactly opposite
"course, and so making the previous manœuvre of no effect."

I think that when the *Kwang Tung* saw again all the three lights
of the *Ngapoota* at what Captain Cobb estimated as a distance of about
half a mile the ships were still under the end on Regulation, but that
that Regulation could not of course override the provisions of Regulation 18.

That the *Ngapoota* in starboarding her helm when she did was
quite in the wrong I can feel no doubt, but the question I have to ask
myself is whether any blame is also to be attributed to the *Kwang Tung*.
If the ships were under the end on rule when the three lights of the
Ngapoota again became visible I do not think that in putting her helm
hard-a-port the *Kwang Tung* committed any fault if the engines were
stopped and reversed soon enough.

Now the first thing I have to remark here is that I believe most
if not all of the estimates of time which have been given us by the
witnesses must be received with considerable caution. Some of the
witnesses I think have evidently not much capacity for naming short
periods of time and with regard to others I do not think estimates of
seconds and minutes formed in respect of moments of great excitement when the mind was fully occupied with something else can be
very exactly relied on.

It seems to me however from the plan produced by and the cal-
culations made on behalf of the defendants, that at the time the three
lights of the *Ngapoota* again became visible to the *Kwang Tung* the

LAW, J

1894.

THE OWNERS OF
THE S.S.
"KWANG TUNG"
V.
THE OWNERS OF
THE S.S.
"NGAPOOTA."

former must have been really nearer to the *Kwang Tung* than Captain Cobb seems to have supposed. Now at the pace the ships were going, half a mile between the ships would have been covered in a little more than a minute and a half, and if the ships were as I believe a good deal less than half a mile apart it would of course take less time to cover the distance between them, although of course we must take into account one fact that it was not the direct distance between the two ships that had to be covered but portions of two circles up to the point of contact.

According to the evidence I believe that at the time the collision occurred the engines of the *Kwang Tung* had not only been stopped but were actually going full speed astern. The engineer says that it takes about 30 seconds to change the engines from full speed ahead to full speed astern, and that at the time of the collision they had made twenty or thirty revolutions astern. Under these circumstances in view of the evidence I believe the order to stop the engines and go astern was given within a minute of the three lights of the *Ngapoota* becoming visible to the *Kwang Tung*.

In the case of the *Emmy Haase* (L. R. 9 P. D 88,) Mr. Justice Butt said " compliance with rule 18 at the very moment when danger becomes " apparent is not necessary ; for a man must have time to consider " whether he should reverse or not. The Court is not bound to hold " that a man should exercise his judgment instantaneously, a short, " but a very short time must be allowed him for this purpose."

Applying the principle above referred to in this case, it seems to me no fault can be found with Captain Cobb for not stopping and reversing sooner. Even Captain Busk says that if he on the *Kwang Tung* had seen the three lights of the *Ngapoota* again, as described, he should have waited to see what the *Ngapoota* was doing. Captain Cobb did not at once when he saw the three lights of the *Ngapoota* stop and reverse the engines, he required a little time to think, but I think he only took a little time and so little time that no blame is to be attached to him for not stopping and reversing sooner.

For these reasons I think all blame for the collision is to be attached to the *Ngapoota* and none to the *Kwang Tung*.

Solicitors for the S. S. *Kwang Tung*,—*Hogan and Adams*.
Solicitors for the S. S. *Ngapoota*,—*Logan and Ross*.

STRAITS SETTLEMENTS

SOH SONG KOK

v.

LOW GUAN SWEE.

MALACCA.

Practice—Powers of Registrar—Civil Procedure Ordinance Secs. 16 and 270—"It shall be Lawful"—Summons for security for costs—Abuse of process of Court.

Where a Summons is taken out returnable before the Registrar in the absence of a Judge under Section 16 of the Civil Procedure Ordinance, the Registrar may under Section 270 of the same Ordinance refer the matter to a Judge.

Where a plaintiff, an alien, has no property in the Colony and the claim in the writ is different to that disclosed by the affidavits. the Court may order him to give security for costs.

COX, C. J.

1894.

Dec. 13.

THIS was Defendant's Summons for security for costs issued under s. 16 s.s. 10 of the Civil Procedure Ordinance and was referred by the Registrar to a Judge under s. 270.

Groom for the Defendant asked that the reference might be dismissed or sent back to the Registrar. Sec. 270 refers only to summons made returnable before the Registrar from orders on which there is an appeal to the Judge within 4 days. The distinction between the two sections is obvious. Under Section 270 when the Registrar has made his order he is *functus officio*. He has acted upon a Summons returnable before himself—summonses under this Section are in trivial matters. Under s. 16 the Summons is returnable before the Court. The Registrar then in the absence of a Judge has a Judge's powers in the important matters set out in section 16 and its subsections. After making his order he is not *functus officio* for on due cause shewn, he may alter vary or discharge it and the litigant has then a month in which to appeal. He is intended to act, not to refer; the Judge may be absent from Malacca for three months. Section 16 is a reproduction of Section 42 of the Courts Ordinance. The words of Section 16 "It shall be lawful," imply the posession of a power which the rules and principles of law require the Registrar to exercise in the absence of a Judge. It is admitted that these words in their primary signification are permissive and enabling only but when coupled with a public duty they are directory. When the power is coupled with a duty, enabling words have a compulsory meaning. The Registrar has refused to perform the judicial duty assigned him in the absence of a judge from the Settlement. He quoted *Reg. v. Tithe Commissioners* (14 Q. B. 470) *Julius v. Bishop of Oxford* (L. R. 5 App. Cas. 214). In any case the words "to refer" in section 270 cannot mean to refer the matter to a judge at the next Malacca Civil Sitting in ten or twelve weeks' time. The power given under Section 22 of the Courts Ordinance to transfer Malacca business to Singapore cannot be exercised without loss of time and considerable expense. The papers should be sent on at once.

[*COX C. J.* held that sections 16 and 270 should be read together and that the Registrar has power to refer.]

Groom.—Then there should be an order for security for costs on the facts set out in the affidavits. The Plaintiff is an alien. It was manifest by the endorsement on the writ of summons that Plaintiff had no cause of action. It was not a *bona fide* action or one in which the Plaintiff could possibly succeed but frivolous and vexatious and was an abuse of process of the Court. The Supreme Court has inherent jurisdiction to see that its process is not abused and can direct a stay of proceedings or security for costs in any cause or matter, pending before it if it think fit. He quoted

Metropolitan Bank v. Pooley (L. R. 10 App. Cas. 210.)

Civil Law Ordinance 1878 s. 1 (5.)

Castro v. Murray (L. R. 10 Ex. 213.)

Dawkins v. Prince of Saxe Weimar (L. R. 1. Q. B. D. 499.)

S. Joaquim for Plaintiff. Poverty is no ground for making a Plaintiff give security for costs. It is admitted Plaintiff is an alien.

COX, C. J.

It has been admitted by Mr. Joaquim that the Plaintiff is an alien and that he has no property in the Colony. The claim in the writ is quite different to that disclosed in the affidavits. Upon the facts I think this is a proper case for the Court to direct security for costs to be given in the sum of $150 within 14 days and in the meantime all proceedings are to be stayed. Should security not be given then this defendant be at liberty to enter a judgment of non-suit as against the Plaintiff.

Solicitors for the Plaintiff.—*Joaquim Bros.*

Solicitor for the Defendant.—*S. R. Groom.*